Musician's Handbook of Foreign Terms

Musician's Handbook of Foreign Terms

Containing the English equivalents of approximately 2700 foreign expression marks and directions taken from French, German, Italian, Latin, Portuguese and Spanish scores.

by

Christine Ammer

SCHIRMER BOOKS
A Division of Macmillan Publishing Co., Inc.
NEW YORK

Collier Macmillan Publishers
LONDON

Copyright © 1971 by Schirmer Books
A Division of Macmillan Publishing Co., Inc.

All rights reserved. No part of this book may be reproduced or transmitted in any form or by any means, electronic or mechanical, including photocopying, recording, or by any information storage and retrieval system, without permission in writing from the Publisher.

Schirmer Books
A Division of Macmillan Publishing Co., Inc.
866 Third Avenue, New York, N.Y. 10022

Collier Macmillan Canada, Ltd.

Library of Congress Catalog Card Number: 77-159278

Printed in the United States of America

printing number

       4 5 6 7 8 9 10

Author's Note

Virtually all of the terms in this handbook appear in actual musical scores. The only exceptions are organ stops, and pitch names and names of instruments in the four principal languages (French, German, Italian, Spanish). The terms are listed in strict alphabetical order, letter by letter, up to the comma in the case of inversion. In the case of adjectives, both masculine and feminine forms are given whenever the two are very different or when both are frequently used. When a single term has two or more entirely different meanings, such as *amaramente,* the reader is asked to rely on the context in which the term appears — that is, the style of the score — in order to determine which meaning is intended.

The terms in this book are drawn from some 30,000 scores. Their compilation was greatly assisted by Diana Cole Roberts, without whose patient and conscientious research this work would not have been possible.

Italian Pronunciation

Vowels and diphthongs
a (arte) as in *a*rt, f*a*ther
ai (aiuto) as in f*i*le
ao (Paolo) as in f*ou*l
au (fausto) as in f*ou*l
e (tre) as in p*e*n
i before a consonant (fine) as in k*ee*p, m*ea*n
i before a vowel (piano, pieno, più) as in *y*es, opin*i*on
o (come) as in t*o*pic
u (duro, tutti) as in p*oo*r, t*oo*

Consonants and consonant combinations
c before a, o, u (caro, con, culto) as in *c*an
c, cc before e, i (cento, cima, cuccina) as in *ch*ief
ch (che) as in *c*an
g before a, o, u (gaio, goffo, gusto) as in *g*et
g before e, i (gentile, gioco) as in *g*eneral
gg before e, i (leggere, leggio) as in coura*g*e
gh before e, i (ghezzo, ghiaccio) as in *g*uilt
gl before a, e, o, u (glaciale, glotta) as in *gl*eam
gl before i (gli) as in bri*lli*ant
gn (legno) as opin*i*on
h (hai) as in *h*onor (always silent)
qu (questo) as in *qu*estion
s (secco) as in English (*s*en*s*e) except when between two vowels (mese), then soft as in ro*s*e
sc before e, i (scena, scienza) as in *sh*ade
z, zz may be either hard (zio), as in flo*ts*am, or soft (canzona), as in *z*one

Stress
The primary accent is usually on the next-to-last syllable or on the final vowel where it bears a written accent (città), but there are numerous exceptions.

German Pronunciation

Vowels and diphthongs

A vowel is long when followed by a single consonant (usually), when doubled, or when followed by the letter *h*. A vowel is short when followed by more than one consonant, and, in some short words, when followed by a single consonant.

    long *a, aa, ah* (Vater, Haare, Hahn) as in f*a*ther
    short *a* (Haft) as in b*u*t
    ai, ay (Mai, Mayer) as in m*y*
    au (laut) as in *ou*t
    long *ä, äh* (Mädchen, fähig) as in f*a*te
    short *ä* (Kälte) as b*e*lt, l*e*t
    äu (Fräulein) as in t*oi*l
    long *e, ee, eh* (Segel, Seele, Sehnsucht) as in g*ay*, p*ai*n
    short *e* (Bett) as in y*e*t
    e in unaccented syllables (Glocke) as in op*e*n, *u*pon
    ei, ey (mein, Meyer) as in l*i*ne
    er (fertig) as in *air*, b*are*
    er in unaccented syllables (Diener) as in butt*er*
    eu (heulen) as in *oi*l
    long *i, ie, ih* (hin, schief, ihnen) as in f*ee*l, l*ea*n
    short *i* (mit, binden) as in *i*t
    long *o, oh, oo* (wo, Hohn, Boot) as in qu*o*te, b*oa*t
    short *o* (kommen) pronounced halfway between b*u*t and r*o*d
    long *ö, öh* (böse, Höhle) similar to h*ur*t or h*er* but longer
    short *ö* (Hölle) similar to unaccented fett*er* but shorter
    long *u, uh* (gut, Schuh) as in l*oo*t
    short *u* (und) as in f*oo*t, p*u*t
    long *ü, üh* (trüb, Mühe) similar to saying, with lips shaped for *oo*, the sound *ee* as in k*ee*p
    short *ü, y* (Glück, Typus) similar to saying, with lips shaped for *oo*, the sound of *i* as in l*i*p

Consonants and consonant combinations

    b (baden) as in *b*ath, except at end of word (gab), then pronounced as p, as in ga*p*
    c before e, ä, i, y (Celsius) as in flo*ts*am

c before a, o, u (café, corps) as in *c*an

ch after a, o, u, au (auch, Tuch) pronounced by forcing the breath between tongue and uvula

ch after ei, eu, i (ich, weich) similar to the *h* in whispering *h*uge

ch in words of Greek origin (Chor) as in *ch*orus

d (da) as in *d*ate, except at end of word (Kind), then pronounced as *t*, as in ca*t*

g before vowels (Gabel, gut) as in *g*atè, *g*ive

g at end of word (Tag) pronounced as *k*, as in tac*k*

g in the closing syllables ig, igst, igt (wenig) is pronounced as a *ch* after ei, eu, i (see above)

j (jung) as in *y*es

kn (Knie) pronounced by sounding both *k* and *n* in succession

pf (Pfund) pronounced by sounding both *p* and *f* in succession

ph (Phantasie) as in *ph*onic

ps (Psalmodie) pronounced by sounding both *p* and *s*

qu (Quelle) pronounced by sounding first *k* and then *v*

s at beginning of word or syllable (sagen, rasieren) as in ri*s*e, *z*ero

s at end of word or syllable (das, Kasse) as in *s*un, ma*ss*

sch (schön) as in *sh*ine

sp at beginning of word or syllable (Sprache) pronounced by sounding first *sh* and then *p*

ss, sz (gross, Szene) as in *s*un

st at beginning of word or syllable (stets) pronounced by sounding first *sh* and then *t*

th (Thema) as in *t*ake

tz (sitzen) as in flo*ts*am

v (von) as in *f*ather

w (wo) as in *v*ery

z (zu) as in flo*ts*am, *ts*ar

Stress

The primary accent falls on the stem syllable, usually the first syllable. In words compounded with syllables before the stem (prefixes) the prefix is accented unless it is one of the following, which are never accented: be-, emp-, ent-, er-, ge-, ver-, zer-. In words ending with -ei the accent falls on the last syllable.

French Pronunciation

Vowels and Diphthongs

short *a* (patte) midway between the a in f*a*ther and c*a*t
long *a, â* (tard, âme) as in f*a*ther
ai (faim) as in d*e*bt
an (dans) as in *aw*ning
au (faux) as in g*o*
é (clé) as in f*a*te but more open
è, ê (élève, même) as in d*e*bt but longer
e in unaccented syllables (refrain) as in op*e*n, *a*gain
eau (beau) as in g*o*
ei (feindre) as in d*e*bt
en (enfin) as in *aw*ning
short *eu* (neveu) similar to saying, with lips shaped to sound *oh*, the sound of *e* in b*e*d
long *eu* (nerveuse) similar to saying, with lips shaped to sound *oh*, the sound of *a* in *a*le
euil (feuille) similar to saying, in rapid succession, the sounds *eu* (see above) and *ee*
eur (faveur) as in p*urr* but longer
long *i, î,* (cri, intîme) as in b*ee*f
short *i* (vif, dire) as in m*e*re
in (enfin) as in f*a*n but more nasalized
short *o* (voler) similar to f*o*lly but shorter
long *ô* (rôle) similar to d*o*le
oe (oeuf) same as short *eu* (see above)
oi (bois) as in *wa*nder
on (bonbon) similar to saying d*ong* but with a long *o* (as in ph*o*ne) and with the g nasalized
short *ou* (bourse) as in p*oo*r
long *ou* (tout) as in t*oo*l
short *u* (une) similar to saying, with lips shaped to say *oo*, the sound of *i* as in t*i*p
long *u* (rue, salut) similar to saying, with lips shaped to say *oo*, the sound of *ee* as in k*ee*p
ui (huit) similar to saying, in rapid succession, *oo-ee*

uin (juin) similar to saying, in rapid succession, *oo-an*
un (défunt) similar to saying, in rapid succession, *oh-an*

Consonants and consonant combinations

c before a, o, u (carte, coquette, cul) as in *c*ake

c before e, i (cette, ciel) as in *s*alad

ch (charge) as in *sh*all

g before a, o, u (galant, gout, guide) as in *g*et

g before e, i (gentil, gilet) as in gentle but softer, like the *zh* sound in vi*s*ion

gn (agneau, soigné) similar to the *ny* sound in a*nnu*al

h (hacher) always silent, as in *h*onor

j (juste) like the *zh* sound in vi*s*ion, mira*g*e

qu (qualité) as in *c*anter

s (sec) as in *s*alad, except when between two vowels (raser), then soft as in ri*s*e

v (vif) as in *v*illage

w (wagon) as in *v*illage

x at end of words may be silent (aux) or sounded (six) as in gee*s*e

Liaison

When a word begins with a vowel or with a mute *h*, in most cases it is joined with the last consonant of the preceding word, even when that consonant is followed by a mute *e*. In such instances the final consonant is pronounced as though it were the first letter of the second word, as in *avec elle*, pronounced as ah-vek-el.

Stress

Unlike English, Italian, and German, in French the primary accent tends to fall on the last syllable.

Abbreviations

cap.	capital
e.g.	for example
F.	French
G.	German
It.	Italian
L.	Latin
Port.	Portuguese
Sp.	Spanish

Ornaments and Signs

Musician's Handbook of Foreign Terms

Musician's Handbook of Foreign Terms

A

a (1) (It.) To, from, by. (2) (Sp.) To, at, in, by, of.

à (F.) To, at, in.

ab (G.) Off, meaning organ stops or mutes.

abafando (Port.) Muffled, muted.

abandon, avec (F.) Free, unrestrained, passionate. Also, **abandonné.**

abandono, con (Sp.) (1) Forlorn, yielding. Also, **con abandonamiento.** (2) Unrestrained, passionate.

abbandono, con (It.) Unrestrained, free, passionate.

abbastanza (It.) Enough, rather, e.g., *abbastanza lento,* rather slow.

abbruciante (It.) Fiery.

abdämpfen (G.) To mute (timpani, etc.).

aber (G.) But, e.g., *eilend aber leise,* fast but soft.

abgemessen (G.) In strict time.

abgestossen (G.) Same as DÉTACHÉ.

abnehmend (G.) Diminishing in loudness.

abschwellen (G.) Becoming softer.

absetzen (G.) To separate, either notes or phrases.

abstossen (G.) (1) In violin music, same as DÉTACHÉ. (2) In organ music, to take off a stop.

abstürzend (G.) Dropping sharply, suddenly softer.

abwechseln (G.) To alternate.

accablement, avec (F.) Heavily, very dejected.

accalorandosi (It.) Becoming excited, growing more animated.

accanito (It.) Also, **accanitamente.** (1) Frenzied, furious. (2) Persistent, obstinate.

accarezzevole (It.) Caressing, soothing, affectionate.

accelerando (It.) Becoming faster, Also, **accel.**

accélérant (F.) Becoming faster. Also, **accélérez.**

accent (F.) Expression, e.g., *d'un accent sauvage,* with fierce expression.

accentato (It.) Accented, emphasized, stressed. Also, **accentuare, accentuato, con accentuazione.**

accentué (F.) Accented, marked, stressed.

acceso (It.) Sparkling, brilliant.

acciaccatura (It.) A short grace note.

acciaccato (It.) Pounded, hammered.

accompagnando (It.) Accompanying.

accompagnant, en (F.) Accompanying.

accorato (It.) Sad, melancholy.

accordando, come (It.) As if in unison.

accordo (It.) Chord, e.g., *tenuti gli accordi,* sustain the chords.

accordo, d' (It.) In tune.

accouplé (F.) Coupler, i.e., using a coupler. Also, **accouplez.**

accusé (F.) With emphasis.

acelerando (Sp.) Becoming faster. Also, **acelerar.**

acentuado (Sp.) Emphasized, stressed, accented. Also, **acentuando.**

Achtel (G.) Eighth note, eighth rest.

acusado (Sp.) Attacked.

acuta (It., L.) In organs, a mixture stop that includes a rank of pipes sounding a third higher than the keys played. Also, (G.) **Scharf,** (L.) **vox acuta.**

acuto (It.) (1) High-pitched, shrill. (2) Sharp. (3) Top note.

adagio (It.) A slow tempo, slower than ANDANTE but not as slow as LENTO.

addolcito (It.) Softer, sometimes also slower. Also, **addolcendo.**

adirato (It.) Enraged, angry.

ad libitum (L.) Freely, at will, improvised. Also, **ad lib.**

adoucissant (F.) Becoming gentler and smoother.

aeolina (L.) In organs, a rank of very soft 8-foot string or foundation pipes tuned either slightly sharp or slightly flat.

aeoline (F.) In organs, one of the softest string stops.

aeoline céleste (F.) A very soft undulating organ stop, made up of two ranks of aeoline pipes, one tuned normally and the other slightly sharp.

Aequalprinzipal (G.) In organs, the major 8-foot diapason or principal stop.

aereo (It.) Light, graceful, airy.

aérien (F.) Light, airy.

afectuoso (Sp.) Fondly, with warmth.

affabile (It.) Gentle, pleasing.

affaiblissez (F.) Become softer and weaker. Also, **affaibli.**

affannato (It.) Breathless, hurried, agitated. Also, **affannoso, affannosamente, con affanno.**

affectueusement (F.) Fondly, tenderly.

Affekt, mit (G.) Passionately. Also, **mit Affect.**

affettuoso (It.) Tenderly, with feeling. Also, **con affetto.**

affezione, con (It.) Tenderly, with feeling.

affirmatif (F.) Assertive, definite. Also, **affirmé.**

affolé (F.) Distracted, bewitched, maddened.

affrettando (It.) Hurrying, rushed, pressing on. Also, **affrettare, affrettato.**

agevole (It.) Easy, smooth, fluent.

aggizunione (It.) Same as NACH-SCHLAG.

aggressivo (It.) Bold, forthright.

agiatamente (It.) With ease, unhurried, comfortably.

agíl (Sp.) Nimble, fast, light.

agilità, con (It.) Nimbly, lightly. Also, **agilmente**.

agitato (It.) Excited, restless. Also, **agitando, agitare, con agitazione**.

agité (F.) Excited, restless, fluttering.

agressivement (F.) Forthright, bold.

aigre (F.) Harsh, shrill.

aigu (F.) Sharp, shrill.

ailé (F.) Rapid and light, skimming.

air, à l' (F.) In the air, up, e.g., *pavillon à l'air,* bell (of horn, etc.) in the air.

airoso (Sp.) Graceful, light, lively.

aise, à l' (F.) Comfortably, easily.

ajoutez (F.) Add, interpolate, e.g., add an organ stop.

Akkord (G.) Chord.

Akzent (G.) Accent.

akzentuiert (G.) Accented, emphasized, marked.

al (It.) To the.

alangui (F.) Slowed down, weaker, softer. Also, **en alanguissant**.

alato (It.) Eloquent, lofty.

a la vez (Sp.) At the same time.

a la vez que (Sp.) While.

alcuna (It.) Some, certain.

aleggiare (It.) Fluttering, quivering.

alegre (Sp.) Cheerful, gay. Also, **con alegría**.

alejándose (Sp.) Dying away, becoming distant.

alenti (F.) Slowed down.

alerte (F.) Lively, brisk.

algo (Sp.) Somewhat.

all°, allo. (It.) Short for ALLEGRETTO.

alla, alle, allo (It.) To the.

allant (F.) Lively, bustling.

allargando (It.) Slowing down, becoming broader and sometimes also louder.

alle (G.) All.

allegramente (It.) Cheerfully, gaily.

allègre (F.) Lively, sprightly, gay.

allegretto (It.) A moderately quick tempo, slower than ALLEGRO but faster than ANDANTE.

allegro (It.) A fast, lively tempo, faster than ALLEGRETTO but slower than PRESTO.

allein (G.) Alone, only.

allentando (It.) Slowing down, slackening the tempo.

allez (F.) Go on, proceed.

allmählich (G.) Gradually.

allonger (F.) To slow down, to hold back, to delay.

allontanandosi (It.) Withdrawing, removing.

alma, con (1) (It.) With spirit, soulfully. (2) (Sp.) With vigor.

alourdissez (F.) Make dull and heavy, weigh down. Also, **alourdir**.

als (G.) As.

al seg. (It.) Short for al SEGNO.

als möglich (G.) As possible, e.g., *so schnell als möglich,* as fast as possible.

alterezza, con (It.) Haughtily, proudly.

alto (F.) Viola.

alzando (It.) Rising, becoming louder.

am (G.) By the, on the, e.g., *am Steg,* on the bridge.

amabile (It.) Sweet, loving. Also, **con amabilità.**

amaramente (It.) Also, **con amarezza.** (1) Harshly, sharply. (2) Sadly, painfully.

amer, amère (F.) Harsh, bitter.

amore, con (It.) Fondly, with love, with warm feeling. Also, **amorevole, amoroso, amorosamente.**

amorosa (It.) In organs, a hybrid flute stop. Also, **flauto amabile.**

ampiamente (It.) Broadly. Also, **ampio, con ampiezza.**

ample (F.) Broadly, with dignity. Also, **amplement, avec ampleur.**

amplio (Sp.) Broad, full. Also, **ampliamente.**

an (G.) In organ music, draw a stop.

anacrouse (F.) Upbeat.

analoge (G.) Analogous, same.

anbetend (G.) Worshipful, adoring.

anches (F.) Reeds.

anchura, con (Sp.) (1) Broadly, fully. (2) Comfortably, easily.

ancora (It.) Again.

Andacht, mit (G.) With devotion, prayerfully. Also, **andächtig.**

andante (It.) A moderately slow tempo, faster than ADAGIO but slower than ALLEGRETTO.

andantino (It.) Usually, a tempo slightly faster than ANDANTE (but occasionally, slightly slower than andante is meant).

and^{te} (It.) Short for ANDANTE.

Anfang, vom (G.) From the beginning.

Anfangstempo (G.) Opening tempo. Also, **Anfangszeitmass.**

angenehm (G). Pleasant, comfortable.

angeschlagen (G.) Also, **anschlagen.** (1) Struck, sounded. (2) Touched (strings or keys).

angoisse, avec (F.) With anguish, in a distressed manner. Also, **angoissé.**

angoscia, con (It.) Sorrowful, grieving, anguished. Also, **angoscioso.**

ängstlich (G.) Hesitantly, nervously.

anhalten (G.) To hold; same as FERMATA.

anhaltend (G.) Constant, continuous, e.g., *anhaltend laut,* constantly loud.

ánima, con (Sp.) Soulful, with feeling.

animación, con (Sp.) Lively, bustling.

animado (Sp.) Lively.

animato (It.) Lively, animated, spirited. Also, **con anima.**

animé (F.) Lively, animated. Also,

en animant.

anmutig (G.) Graceful. Also, **mit Anmut.**

anreissen (G.) In string playing, a forceful attack.

ansante (It.) Breathless, panting, gasping.

anschlagen (G.) (1) To strike, to sound. (2) To touch (a key or string).

anschliessend, gleich (G.) Immediately adjoining, i.e., continue without pause.

anschwellend (G.) Becoming louder. Also, **anschwellen.**

ansiedad, con (Sp.) Anxiously, worriedly.

ansioso (It.) Eagerly, longingly, impatiently. Also, (It., Sp.) **con ansia.**

anstimmen (G.) (1) To tune. (2) To begin to sing.

anstürmend (G.) Rushing on.

antebrazo, con el (Sp.) With the forearm.

Anteil, mit (G.) In proportion, appropriately.

anterior (Sp.) Preceding, former, earlier, e.g., *ritmo anterior,* the preceding rhythm.

antes que (Sp.) Before, earlier than.

antwortend (G.) Answering. Also, **antworten.**

anwachsend (G.) Becoming louder.

apagado (Sp.) Softly, without emphasis, muffled, muted.

apaisé (F.) Calm, quiet. Also, **en s'apaisant.**

apasionado (Sp.) Impassioned.

à peine (F.) Hardly, scarcely.

aperto (It.) (1) Open, referring to open notes (horn), open pipes (organ). (2) Obvious, clear, e.g., *allegro aperto,* a definite allegro tempo. (3) In piano music, depress damper pedal.

Apfelregal (G.) In organs, an 8-foot regal stop.

a poco (Sp.) Immediately, soon, shortly.

apoyado (Sp.) With emphasis.

appassionato (It.) Passionate, ardent. Also, **appassionatamente.**

appena (It.) Scarcely, very slightly, e.g., *appena ritardando,* slowing down very slightly, *appena toccato,* scarcely played (i.e., very soft).

appesantendo (It.) Becoming heavier and broader.

appoggiando (It.) (1) Emphasized, reinforced. (2) Supporting, accompanying, e.g., *appoggiando il canto,* accompanying the melody (or vocal part).

appressando (It.) Approaching, coming closer, becoming louder.

appuntato (It.) Sharply, precisely.

appuyé (F.) With emphasis.

après (F.) After.

âpreté, avec (F.) Harshly, violently. Also, **âpre.**

apurando (Sp.) Hurrying, pressing on.

arcata (It.) Bowing.

arcato (It.) Bowed.

archet (F.) Bow.

arco (It.) (1) The bow, or use the bow. (2) Neck of a harp.

ardente (It.) Passionate, fervent, impetuous.

ardito (It.) Bold. Also, **arditamente.**

ardore, con (It.) With great warmth, fervently.

argentin (F.) Silvery, clear, bell-like.

argentino (It.) Same as ARGENTIN.

arioso (It.) (1) Melodic, singing. (2) An expressive vocal style.

armónicos (Sp.) Harmonics.

armonioso (It.) Tuneful, harmonious.

arpa (It., Sp.) Harp.

arpégé (F.) Like a broken chord (arpeggio). Also, **arpèges.**

arpeggiando (It.) Playing broken chords.

arpeggieren (G.) Same as ARPEGGIANDO.

arpeggio (It.) A broken chord (with notes played in succession instead of together).

arpegio (Sp.) Same as ARPEGGIO.

arraché (F.) Forceful pizzicato.

arrastiando (Sp.) Dragging out, slow.

arrêt (F.) Stop, halt.

arrêtez (F.) Stop, e.g., *arrêtez l'archet,* stop bowing.

arrogamment (F.) Haughtily, proudly.

arrullo (Sp.) (1) Whispering, murmuring. (2) A lullaby.

articolando (It.) Pronouncing clearly and distinctly, articulating.

articulé (F.) Distinct, articulated.

-artig (G.) In the manner of, like, e.g., *kadenzartig,* like a cadenza.

artig (G.) Neat, pleasing, polite. Also, **artiglich.**

aspero (Sp.) Harsh, gruff.

aspro (It.) Harsh, rough, sharp. Also, **aspramente.**

assai (It.) Much, very, e.g., *allegro assai,* very fast.

assez (F.) Quite, enough, fairly, e.g., *assez vite,* fairly fast.

assombrissant, en s' (F.) Darkening, becoming gloomy.

assordire (It.) Deafening, very loud.

assorto (It.) Preoccupied.

astioso (It.) Envious, spiteful.

astuto (It.) Wide awake, bright, sharp.

ataque (Sp.) Attack.

Atem (G.) Breath.

atemlos (G.) Breathless.

a tempo (It.) See TEMPO, A.

attacca (It.) Continue without a pause. Also, **attacca subito.**

attaque (F.) Attack, touch.

attarder, s' (F.) To delay, to linger. Also, **attardé.**

attendre (F.) Wait, pause.

attendri (F.) Gently, tenderly.

atténué (F.) Weaker, softer.

au, aux (F.) At the, to the.

auf (G.) (1) Open up, e.g., *Schalltrichter auf,* bells (of horns) up. (2) On, in, at, e.g., *auf ♩ = 66,* at (a tempo of) 66 half notes per minute.

aufbäumend (G.) Surging up, swelling.

auffahrend (G.) Passionate, vehement.

aufflackernd (G.) Flaring up, flickering, wavering.

aufflammend (G.) Flaring up.

aufgeblasen (G.) Arrogant, haughty.

aufgebracht (G.) Furious.

aufgeregt (G.) Excited, agitated.

aufhalten (G.) To hold back, to slow down.

aufjauchzend (G.) Shouting with joy.

auflebend (G.) Reviving, becoming livelier.

aufrauschend (G.) Swelling, becoming louder.

aufschluchzend (G.) Sobbing.

aufschreiend (G.) Crying out, shrieking.

Aufschwung (G.) With enthusiasm, soaring.

Aufstrich (G.) Up-bow.

Auftakt (G.) Upbeat.

Auftritt (G.) Scene.

augmentant, en (F.) Becoming louder. Also, **augmenter.**

aumentando (It., Sp.) Becoming louder.

aún (Sp.) Yet, still.

aus (G.) Out of.

ausbrechend (G.) Bursting out, explosive.

ausbreiten (G.) Becoming broader.

Ausdruck, mit (G.) With expression. Also, **ausdrucksvoll.**

ausdruckslos (G.) Without emphasis or expression, monotonous.

ausgeglichen (G.) Smooth, well-balanced, steady.

ausgelassen (G.) Exuberant, boisterous.

aushalten (G.) To sustain.

ausholen (G.) To attack.

ausklingen (G.) To die away.

ausladend (G.) Projecting, with a full tone.

auslaufen (G.) To conclude, to end.

Ausschwung (G.) Swing, momentum.

äusserst (G.) To the utmost, extremely, e.g., *äusserst ruhig,* as quiet as possible.

aussi bien que (F.) As well as.

aussingen (G.) To sing to the end.

aussi peu que (F.) As little as.

aussi — que possible (F.) As — as possible, e.g., *aussi doux que possible,* as soft as possible, *aussi fort que possible,* as loud as possible.

ausströmen (G.) To stream forth, to gush out.

autant que (F.) As much as.

autoritaire (F.) Commanding, decisive.

avant (F.) Before, in front of.

avantbras, avec l' (F.) With the forearm.

avanzar (Sp.) To push forward, to press on.

avec (F.) With.

avisée (F.) Prudent, careful.

avivar (Sp.) To speed up.

à volonté (F.) At will, freely, at the performer's discretion.

avvicinandosi (It.) Approaching.

avvilimento, con (It.) Dejected, discouraged, humiliated. Also, **avvilito.**

avvivando (It.) Becoming livelier.

azione, con (It.) With action, staged.

B

bacchantisch (G.) Reveling.

bacchetta (It.) Drumstick, beater.

badin (F.) Playful, droll.

badinant, en (F.) In fun, jestingly.

baigné de pédales (F.) Pedal throughout.

baixo (Port.) Bass.

baja, bajo (Sp.) Lower, e.g., *8a baja*, an octave lower.

bajón (Sp.) Bassoon.

balancé (F.) (1) Evenly. (2) A dance step.

baldanza, con (It.) Boldly, confidently.

ballabile (It.) Dancelike.

ballmässig (G.) Dancelike.

ballo (It.) Dance, e.g., *tempo di ballo*, in dance tempo.

balzando (It.) Bouncy, springy.

barbaro (It.) Fierce, savage.

barcollante (It.) Tottering, staggering.

Barpfeife (G.) In organs, a reed stop of the regal group.

Baryton (G.) In organs, a soft 8-foot reed stop.

basse marquée, la (F.) The bass (part) emphasized.

Bassgeige (G.) Double bass.

Bassklarinette (G.) Bass clarinet.

basso (It.) Bass (part or voice), e.g., *basso marcato*, emphasize the bass.

basson (F.) Bassoon.

bastante (Sp.) Enough, rather, fairly, e.g., *bastante tranquilo*, rather calm.

batido (Sp.) Pounded, struck with force.

battement (F.) (1) Acoustical beats. (2) Formerly, an ornament.

battere (It.) (1) Beat a drum (or other percussion instrument). (2) Emphasize, stress insistently.

batterie (F.) (1) Percussion section. (2) Drum roll.

battre (F.) To beat, to pant, to throb.

battre le mesure (F.) To beat time.

battuta (It.) (1) Measure, bar. (2) Beat, especially the accented first beat of a measure, e.g., *ritmo di tre battute*, a rhythm of three beats (one per measure).

battuta, a (It.) Return to strict time.

battuta d'aspetto (It.) One-measure rest.

battuta in aria (It.) Upbeat.

battuta in terra (It.) Downbeat.

Bauerflöte (G.) In organs, a stopped wooden flute stop.

beaucoup (F.) Very, quite, much.

Becken (G.) Cymbals.

bedächtig (G.) Unhurried, deliberate.

bedeutend (G.) Considerably, definitely, e.g., *bedeutend laut*, quite loud.

bedrohlich (G.) Threatening, threateningly.

Begeisterung, mit (G.) Enthusiastically, with spirit. Also, **begeistert**.

begleiten (G.) To accompany. Also, **Begleitung**, accompaniment.

behäbig (G.) Easily, comfortably.

behaglich (G.) Comfortably, with ease.

behende (G.) Nimbly, quickly.

behutsam (G.) Careful, wary, gingerly.

beide (G.) Both, e.g., *beide Pedal*, both pedals.

Beifall klatschend (G.) Applauding.

beinahe (G.) Almost, nearly.

beleben (G.) To revive, to animate.

belebt (G.) Brisk, animated. Also, **belebend**.

belliqueux (F.) Martial.

bem (Port.) Well, thoroughly.

bemolle (It.) Flat, e.g., *A bemolle*, A-flat.

ben, bene (It.) Well, quite, e.g., *ben marcato*, quite accented, *ben ritmato*, quite rhythmic (with an even beat).

ben sentito (It.) Warmly, strongly.

bequem (G.) Comfortable, easy.

berceur (F.) Lullaby. Also, **berceuse**.

beruhigt (G.) Calm, quiet. Also, **beruhigend**.

beschaulich (G.) Meditative, quiet, tranquil.

beschleunigen (G.) To speed up, to increase the tempo. Also, **beschleunigt, beschleunigend**.

beschwingt (G.) Light and swift, flying.

beschwörend (G.) Entreating, imploring.

besinnlich (G.) Thoughtful, reflective.

besorgt (G.) Anxious, disquieted. Also, **mit Besorgnis**.

bestiale (It.) Brutal, cruel.

bestimmt (G.) With decision.

betont (G.) Stressed, emphasized, accented. Also, **mit Betonung**.

Betonungen, ohne (G.) Without accents.

beträchtlich (G.) Considerably, a good deal.

bewegt (G.) Animated, with motion. Also, **mit Bewegung**.

bianca (It.) Half note.

biecamente (It.) Grimly, sullenly.

bien (F.) Well, thoroughly.

bién (Sp.) Well, quite, very.

bis (1) (G.) Up to, until, e.g., *bis zum Schluss*, up to the end. (2) (L.) Twice, indicating a repeat.

bisbigliato (It.) Whispered. Also, **bisbigliando**, whispering.

bischen, ein (G.) A little, e.g., *ein bischen schneller*, a little faster.

biscroma (It.) Thirty-second note.

bissig (G.) Ferocious, biting, sharp.

bittend (G.) Pleading.

bizarre (F.) Strange, fanciful.

bizarro (It.) Unusual, freakish, capricious.

blanca (Sp.) Half note.

blanche (F.) Half note.

blandamente (It.) Gently, softly.

blando (Sp.) Tenderly, gently.

blass (G.) Colorless, pale, unemphasized, e.g., *mit blassem Ton,* with a colorless, flat tone.

bleiben (G.) To stay, to remain, e.g., *im Tempo bleiben,* remain in (strict) time.

bleich (G.) Same as BLASS.

Blockflöte (G.) (1) Recorder. (2) In organs, an open metal flute stop.

boca cerrada (Sp.) With the mouth closed, humming.

bocca chiusa, a (It.) Humming.

Bogen (G.) Bow.

Bogenspitze, mit (G.) With the point of the bow.

bois (F.) (1) Wood, stick of the bow. (2) Woodwind instruments.

boîte (F.) In organs, the swell, e.g., *boîte fermée,* swell closed.

bombarde (F.) In organs, a powerful chorus reed stop.

bombarde quinte (F.) In organs, a chorus reed stop.

bombardino (Sp.) Euphonium.

bombardon (F.) In organs, a chorus reed stop.

bombastisch (G.) Inflated, conceited.

bombo (Sp.) Bass drum.

bonarietà, con (It.) With good nature, amiably.

bondissant (F.) Skipping, bounding.

bonheur, avec (F.) Happily.

bonté, avec (F.) Kindly, with good will.

borbottando (It.) Muttering, grumbling.

Bordunalflöte (G.) In organs, an open wooden flute stop. Also, **Portunalflöte**.

bouche (F.) Mouth.

bouché (F.) Stopped note (in horns, etc.).

bourdon (F.) (1) A bagpipe drone or sympathetic string. (2) Refrain. (3) In organs, an important stopped flute stop. Also, **bourd.** (4) The largest bell of a carillon.

Bourdonecho (F., G.) In organs, a very soft stopped flute stop. Also, **echo bourdon**.

bourrasque (F.) Angry, stormy.

bousculer (F.) To hurry, to become agitated. Also, **bousculade**.

Bratsche (G.) Viola.

Bravour, mit (G.) Brilliantly, with dash, with great skill.

bravoure, avec (F.) Bravely, gallantly.

bravura, con (It.) With great technical skill, in a virtuoso manner.

bref, brève (F.) Concise, brief.

breit (G.) (1) Broad, same as LARGO. (2) Broadly, e.g., *breit gestrichen,* broadly bowed.

breve (It.) Brief, concise; appearing over ⌢, short pause. Also see BREVE, ALLA.

breve, alla (It.) Twice as fast.

brilhante (Port.) Brilliant, sparkling.

brillant (F.) Brilliant, showy, sparkling.

brillante (It.) Sparkling, spirited.

brincando (Sp.) Skipping, bounding.

brindisi (It.) Drinking song.

brio, con (It.) Vigorously, with fire. Also, **brioso.**

brisé (F.) Short detached bow strokes.

brivido (It.) Shivering, trembling.

brouillé de pédale (F.) In organ playing, a mixture of pedal stops.

brumeux (F.) Misty, veiled.

brummen (G.) To hum. Also, **Brummstimme.**

brusca, brusco (Sp.) Roughly, harshly.

brusco (It.) Sharply, curtly, abruptly. Also, **bruscamente.**

brusque (F.) Sharp, abrupt, sudden. Also, **brusquement.**

brutale (It.) Savage, fierce, cruel.

bugle à pistons (F.) Flugelhorn.

buccina (1) (It.) In organs, a chorus reed stop. (2) (L.) Trumpet.

buffa, buffo (It.) Comic, clownish.

buio (It.) Dark.

burla, alla (It.) Playful, joking.

burlesco (It.) Jesting, light.

burlesk (G.) Mock-heroic.

C

caché (F.) Hidden, discreet, subtle.

cada (Sp.) Each, every.

cadencé (F.) (1) Measured, rhythmic. (2) Trilled.

cadendo (It.) Becoming softer.

cadenza (It.) (1) A cadenza, florid passage. (2) Cadence, close.

cadenzato (It.) In a regular rhythm, measured.

caisse roulante (F.) Tenor drum. Also, **caisse sourde.**

calando (It.) Becoming softer and slower.

calcando (It.) (1) Forcefully, pressing on. (2) Imitating, copying.

caldo (It.) Heated, passionate.

calmando (It.) Quieting down, subsiding. Also, **calmandosi, calmato.**

calmant, en se (F.) Becoming calm, tranquil. Also, **calmer, calmez.**

calme (F.) Tranquil, still, quiet.

calore, con (It.) With warmth, fervent, impetuous. Also, **caloroso.**

caminando (Sp.) Same as CAMMINANDO.

camminando (It.) Moving on, flowing.

campana (It.) (1) Bell, chime. Also, **campane,** bells, (orchestral) chimes. (2) The bell of a wind instrument, e.g., *campane in aria,* with the bells up. (3) In organs, a brilliant high flute or foundation stop. Also, **Zimbelflöte.**

campanas (Sp.) Chimes.

campanette (It.) Glockenspiel.

candeur, avec (F.) Openly, ingenuously, simply.

cantabile (It.) In a singing style, lyrical, melodious, flowing. Also, **cant.,** (It., Sp.) **cantando.**

cantando (Sp.) (1) Same as CANTABILE. (2) Singing.

cantilena (It.) (1) Lullaby. (2) Melodious. (3) A monotonous, sing-song style of performance.

canto (It.) (1) Song. (2) Singing, vocal part. (3) Soprano (treble) part.

capo (It.) Beginning, e.g., *da capo al fine,* from the beginning to the end, *da capo al segno* (𝄋), from the beginning to the sign. Also, part of abbreviation D.C. (da capo).

capriccioso (It.) Fanciful, freely.

caprichosamente (Port., Sp.) Fanciful, whimsical.

capricieux (F.) Fanciful, playful.

carattere, in (It.) In character, typical, appropriate.

caressant (F.) Tender, soothing.

carezzando (It.) Loving, affectionate. Also, **carezzoso.**

carezzevole (It.) Coaxing, caressing, wheedling.

caricato (It.) Heightened, intensified, exaggerated.

caricaturale (It.) Caricatured, over-exaggerated.

carillon (F.) (1) Glockenspiel. (2) In organs, a mixture stop. Also, **Glockenspiel.**

casi (Sp.) Almost, nearly, e.g., *casi f,* almost forte (loud).

cassa rullante (It.) Tenor drum.

castañuelas (Sp.) Castanets.

cedendo (It.) Yielding, slowing down.

cédez (F.) Slow down and become softer. Also, **céder.**

cediendo (Sp.) Slowing down.

celere (It.) Swift, rapid.

céleste (F.) (1) Heavenly, divine, otherworldly. (2) In organs, an undulating beating stop, usually made up of two ranks of deliberately mistuned pipes, e.g., **dolce céleste, gemshorn céleste, gamba céleste,** etc. Also see VOIX CÉLESTE.

celestina (It.) In organs, a very small-scaled open flute stop.

cembalo (G., It.) Harpsichord,

centro, al (It.) At the center (e.g., of a drum).

chaleur, avec (F.) With warmth, fervently. Also, **chaleureux.**

chalumeau (F.) (1) An obsolete form of clarinet. (2) The high register of modern clarinets. (3) In organs, same as SCHALMEI.

chamade (F.) In organs, same as TROMPETTE EN CHAMADE.

chant (F.) (1) Song. (2) Melody, theme.

chantant (F.) In a singing, melodious style. Also, **chanté.**

chanterelle (F.) Highest string (in violins, etc.)

chaque (F.) Each, every.

charme, avec (F.) With charm, gracefully.

chatoyant (F.) Brilliant, showy.

chaud (F.) Warmly, with fervor.

chauffez (F.) Become faster, press on.

cheto (It.) Quiet, hushed.

chevalet, au (F.) On the bridge (of violins, etc.).

chevrotant (F.) Quivering, trembling.

chiaro (It.) Clear, bright, distinct. Also, **chiaramente.**

chiassoso (It.) Noisy, babbling, creating a din.

chitarra (It.) Guitar.

chiusa, chiuso (It.) Closed.

choeur (F.) Choir.

chrétiennement (F.) Charitably.

chuchoté (F.) Whispered.

cierta, cierto (Sp.) Certain, definite, positive.

címbalo (Sp.) Cymbal.

cinelli (It.) Cymbals.

cinglant (F.) Harsh, grating.

circa (It., L.) About, approximately, e.g., *circa ♩ = 54,* at approximately (the tempo of) 54 quarter notes per minute.

cistre (F.) Zither.

clair (F.) Clear, bright, distinct. Also, **clairement.**

clairon (F.) (1) Bugle. (2) In organs, a trumpet stop. Also, **clarion, trumpet clarion.**

clairon harmonique (F.) In organs, an octave chorus reed stop with a powerful tone. Also, **clarion harmonic, harmonic clarion.**

clarabella (It.) In organs, an open flute stop.

clarinete (Sp.) Clarinet.

clarinette (F.) Clarinet.

clarinette basse (F.) Bass clarinet.

clarinetto (It.) Clarinet.

claro (Sp.) Clear, distinct, pure.

clarone (It.) Bass clarinet. Also, **clarinetto basso.**

clavecin (F.) Harpsichord.

clavicembalo (It.) Harpsichord.

clavicordio (Sp.) Harpsichord.

clavier (F.) Keyboard, manual.

clignant de l'oeil (F.) Winking.

coda (It.) End, concluding passage.

col, colla, colle (It.) With the.

colère, avec (F.) Angrily, with passion, furiously.

colpo di lingua (It.) Tonguing.

com (Port.) With.

come (It.) How, like, as, e.g., *come un brivido,* like a shudder, *come prima,* like the first time, *come sopra,* as above.

cómico (Sp.) Droll, humorous.

comienzo (Sp.) Beginning, opening, e.g., *en el tempo de comienzo,* in the opening tempo.

comique (F.) Comical, humorous.

comme (F.) Like, as, as if.

commodément (F.) Easily, comfortably.

commosso (It.) Irritated, annoyed.

como (Sp.) As, like, in the manner of, e.g., *tan lento como sea pueda,* as slow as possible.

cómodante (Sp.) Comfortably, easily. Also, **cómodo.**

comodo (It.) Comfortable, easy, unhurried.

compasso (Port.) (1) Time, meter. (2) Measure, bar.

completo (It.) Wholly, entirely.

compter (F.) To count, e.g., *compter à la double-croche,* to count from (to) the sixteenth note.

con (It., Sp.) With, e.g., (It.) *con calore,* with fervor.

concentrando (It.) Concentrating, condensing, becoming faster.

concentré (F.) Concentrated, dense.

concertato (It.) (1) Soloists, especially those alternating with the full orchestra in a concerto grosso. Also, **concertino, concertante.** (2) Conducted. (3) Scored, orchestrated.

concitato (It.) Excited, agitated, usually in fast tempo. Also, **concitando, con concitazione.**

concluir (Sp.) To end, conclusion.

con esp. (It.) Short for **con espressione;** see ESPRESSIVO.

confus (F.) Vague, indistinct.

contemplativo (It.) Dreamy, meditative.

continu (F.) Continued, maintained. Also, **continué.**

continuo (It.) Continuous bass accompaniment, especially as found in baroque music. Also, **basso continuo.**

contrabajo (Sp.) Double bass, contrabass.

contrabajón (Sp.) Contrabassoon.

contrabasso (It.) Double bass.

contra bombarde (L. + F.) In organs, a deep-toned chorus reed stop.

contra bourdon (L. + F.) In organs, same as SOUBASSE.

contra dulciana (It.) In organs, a very soft foundation stop.

contrafagotto (It.) (1) Contrabassoon. (2) In organs, a low-pitched reed stop.

contra gamba (It.) In organs, a low-pitched string stop. Also, **Grossgamba.**

Contra Posaune (G.) In organs, a low-pitched, loud chorus reed stop.

contra viola (It.) In organs, a string stop.

contra violone (It.) In organs, a bass string stop. Also, **bass violin, contre viole, double bass, violin bass, violone.**

contrebasse (F.) Double bass, contrabass.

contrebasse à pistons (F.) Bass tuba.

contrebasson (F.) Contrabassoon.

contre viole (F.) In organs, same as CONTRA VIOLONE.

coperto (It.) Covered, muted

copula (L.) In organs, a stop designed to blend the tones of other stops.

cor (F.) Horn, French horn.

corale (It.) (1) Choral, pertaining to a choir or its music. (2) Chorale (the musical form).

cor anglais (F.) (1) English horn. (2) In organs, an 8-foot reed stop whose tone resembles that of the orchestral English horn.

corchea (Sp.) Eighth note.

corda (It.) String. Also see TRE CORDE, UNA CORDA.

cor d'amour (F.) In organs, same as CORNO D'AMORE.

cor de basset (F.) In organs, same as CORNO DI BASSETTO.

cor de chasse (F.) In organs, same as WALDHORN.

cor de nuit (F.) In organs, same as NACHTHORN.

corneta (Sp.) Cornet.

cornet à bouquin (F.) Cornett.

cornet à pistons (F.) Cornet.

cornet de récit (F.) In organs, a compound stop of unusually prominent tone.

cornet des bombardes (F.) In organs, a compound stop made up of several ranks of loud, open diapason pipes.

cornet des violes (F.) In organs, a compound stop made up of several ranks of string pipes.

cornetta (It.) Cornet.

cornetto (It.) Cornett.

corno (It.) Horn, French horn.

corno d'amore (It.) In organs, a solo reed stop. Also, **cor d'amour.**

corno di bassetto (It.) (1) Basset horn. (2) In organs, an 8-foot manual reed stop whose tone is similar to that of the basset horn. Also, **cor de basset.**

corno di caccia (It.) In organs, same as WALDHORN.

corno inglés (Sp.) English horn. Also, **cuerno inglés.**

corno inglese (It.) English horn.

corona (It.) (1) Pause. (2) The sign for the fermata (⌢). Also, **lunga corona.**

corrente (It.) (1) Rapid, flowing. (2) A dance similar to the courante.

correr (Sp.) Fast.

correre, senza (It.) Without hurrying.

corta, corto (It., Sp.) Short, brief, concise.

coulé (F.) A slide, similar to a glissando.

coup de vent, comme un (F.) Like a gust of wind, breathy.

courante (F.) (1) Running, rapid, flowing. (2) An old dance.

courroux (F.) Wrath, anger.

court (F.) Short, brief, concise.

crepitante (It.) Crackling, rustling.

crescendo (It.) Becoming louder, swelling. Also, **cresc., cres.**

crespo (It.) Rippling.

cri, comme un (F.) Like an outcry.

cristalino (Sp.) Clear, bright, transparent.

cristallin (F.) Clear, silvery.

cristallino (It.) Clear, bright, pure.

croche (F.) Eighth note.

croisez les mains (F.) Cross the hands.

croma (It.) Eighth note.

cromorne (F., It.) (1) In organs, same as KRUMMHORN. (2) The crumhorn (obsolete woodwind instrument).

cuadro (Sp.) Four.

cuerda (Sp.) String (of violins, etc.).

cullando (It.) Rocking, soothing.

cupo (It.) Gloomy, deep, with a dark tone. Also, **con voce cupa.**

cymbales (F.) Cymbals.

D

d' (F., It.) Of.

da, dal, dalla, dalle, dall' (It.) Of the.

dämonisch (G.) Devilish, fiendish, wild.

Dämpfer (G.) Mute, e.g., *mit Dämpfer,* with mute, *Dämpfer weg,* without mute.

dans (F). In.

dansant (F). Dancing.

danza, como (Sp.) Dancelike.

das (G.) The.

Daumen (G.) Thumb.

davantage (F.) More, further.

D.C. (It.) Short for da CAPO.

de (F., Sp.) Of, from.

déaccouplé (F.) Uncoupled, separated.

début (F.) Beginning.

déchirant (F.) Heartrending, piercing.

décidé (F.) Firm, resolute.

decisivo (It.) Decisive, firm.

deciso (It.) Bold, forceful.

declamato (It.) Recited, spoken.

déclamé (F.) In a declamatory style.

decrescendo (It.) Becoming softer. Also, **decr., decresc.**

défaillant (F.) Giving way, feeble, dying away.

défi, avec (F.) With defiance, challenging.

degli (It.) Of the.

dehnen (G.) To broaden, to prolong.

dehors, en (F.) Emphasized, standing out, accented.

deixa (Port.) Let, allow, e.g., *deixa vibrar,* let (continue to) sound.

dejad (Sp.) Same as DEIXA. Also, **dejar.**

deklamieren (G.) (1) To recite. (2) To perform as a recitative.

deliberamente (It.) Deliberately, ponderously.

delicadeza, con (Sp.) With refinement, daintily, elegantly. Also, **delicado.**

delicadísimo (Sp.) Highly refined and elegant.

délicat (F.) Smoothly, delicately, daintily. Also, **délicatement.**

delicatamente (It.) Daintily, elegantly. Also, **con delicatezza.**

délices, avec (F.) With delight, happily.

delikat (G.) Delicate, tenderly.

delirando (It.) Raving, wild.

délire, en (F.) Frenzied.

dem (G.) The.

demasiado (Sp.) Too much, excessive.

demi jeu (F.) The softer organ stops.

demi-pause (F.) Half rest.

demi-soupir (F.) Eighth rest.

demi-teinte, en (F.) Half-shaded, subtly shaded.

demi-voix, à (F.) Half-voice, softly.

demuthsvoll (G.) Humbly, modestly. Also, **demütig.**

den (G.) The.

dengoso (Sp.) Affected, over-refined.

de plus en plus (F.) More and more.

deprisa (Sp.) Depressed, pushed down.

der (G.) The.

derb (G.) Robust, rough.

derecha, derecho (Sp.) Right (hand).

derisione, con (It.) Mockingly.

dernier, dernière (F.) Last.

desconsolado (Sp.) Griefstricken, downhearted.

desenfado, con (Sp.) Freely, easily.

désespoir, avec (F.) Despairingly.

desfalleciendo (Sp.) Becoming softer, fading away.

desgarrado (Sp.) Shameless, bold.

desiderato (It.) Desired, welcome.

désinence (F.) Ending, final cadence.

desoladamente (Sp.) Sad, disconsolate.

desolato (It.) Sorrowful, disconsolate. Also, **con desolazione.**

désordonné (F.) Disorderly, confused.

despacio (Sp.) Slowly, deliberately.

dessus (F.) On, over, above, e.g., *main droit dessus,* right hand over (the left).

destacado (Sp.) Emphasized, standing out, accented. Also, **destacando.**

destra (It.) Right (hand).

détaché (F.) In bowing, alternate up- and down- bows.

detención (Sp.) Hold, stop, e.g., *detención todos juncos,* everyone stop together.

détendu (F.) Slackened, slower.

deutlich (G.) Clear, distinct.

deux (F.) Two.

devoto (It.) Dedicated, sincere. Also, **devotamente.**

dezent (G.) Restrained, dignified, moderate.

di (It.) Of, e.g., *in modo di ballo,* in the manner of a dance.

diapason (F.) In organs, a foundation stop that gives the instrument its characteristic tone.

diaphane (F.) Clear, transparent.

die (G.) The.

diesis (It.) Sharp, e.g., *A-diesis,* A-sharp.

diffuso (It.) Blurry, scattered; the opposite of clear and concise.

dignità, con (It.) With dignity, gravely.

dileguando (It.) Growing fainter and fainter.

diluendo (It.) Becoming weaker and softer, fading away.

dim. (It.) Short for DIMINUENDO. Also, **dimin.**

diminuant, en (F.) Becoming softer.

diminuendo (It.) Becoming softer. Also, **dim., dimin.**

dinámica (Sp.) (1) Lively, vibrant. Also, **dynámico.** (2) Dynamics.

di nuovo (It.) Again, anew.

direita (Port.) Right (hand).

discrètement (F.) Cautiously, with reserve.

disinvolto (It.) Freely, easily, deftly.

disminyuendo (Sp.) Same as DIMINUENDO. Also, **disminuir**.

disparaissant, en (F.) Disappearing, fading away.

disperazione, con (It.) Wildly, despairingly, despondently. Also, **disperatamente, disperato**.

disprezzo, con (It.) Contemptuously, scornfully.

distaccato (It.) Detached, separated.

disteso (It.) Extended, broad.

distinct (F.) Clear, distinct.

distinto (It.) Clear, distinct, separate.

div. (It.) Short for DIVISI.

diventando (It.) Becoming, changing to, e.g., *diventando allegro,* becoming fast.

divisi (It.) Indicating separate parts where there normally is only one, e.g., the first violins dividing to play two or more separate parts. Also, **div.**

doigté (F.) Fingering.

dolce (It.) (1) Sweet, smooth, gentle. Also, **dolciato, dol.** (2) In organs, a fairly soft foundation stop.

dolcissimo (It.) (1) As sweet and gentle as possible (see DOLCE). (2) In organs, a very soft foundation stop.

dolent (F.) Mournful, plaintive.

dolente (It.) Sorrowful, mournful.

doloroso (It.) Lamenting, grieving. Also, **con dolore**.

donaire (Sp.) Graceful, elegant. Also, **donairoso, donairosamente**.

dopo (It.) After, beyond.

Doppelflöte (G.) In organs, a stopped flute stop, with two mouths per pipe.

Doppelgedeckt (G.) In organs, a stopped flute stop, with two mouths per pipe.

Doppelgriff (G.) Double stop.

Doppelrohrflöte (G.) In organs, a half-covered flute stop.

Doppelrohrgedeckt (G.) In organs, a half-covered flute stop.

Doppelspitzflöte (G.) In organs, an open flute stop.

doppelt (G.) Twice as, double, e.g., *doppelt so schnell,* twice as fast, *doppelt so langsam,* twice as slow.

doppio (It.) Double, twofold, twice as, e.g., *doppio bemolle,* double flat, *doppio colpo di lingua,* double tonguing, *doppio movimento,* twice as fast, *doppio corda,* double stop.

dos (Sp.) Two, e.g., *dos pedales,* two pedals.

double, le (F.) (1) A repeat. (2) A variation. (3) A 16-foot organ stop.

double-croche (F.) Sixteenth note.

doublette (F.) In organs, a stop made up of two diapason ranks of different pitches.

douce, doux (F.) Soft, gentle, smooth. Also, **doucement, avec douceur**.

douloureux (F.) Sorrowful. Also, **douloureusement**.

dramático (Sp.) Dramatic, emotional.

drammatico (It.) Dramatically, somewhat exaggerated. Also, **drammaticamente, con dramma.**

drängend (G.) Pressing on, hurrying. Also, **drängen, mit Drang.**

dreiteilig (G.) Three-part.

dringend (G.) Urgent, pressing.

drohend (G.) Threatening.

Druck (G.) Pressure, strain, e.g., *ohne jeden Druck,* without straining, easily.

D.S. (It.) Short for dal SEGNO.

du (F.) From the, of the.

due (It.) Two, e.g., *due volte,* two times (twice).

due, in (It.) See IN DUE.

duetto (It.) Duet.

duftig (G.) Sweetly, light.

dulce (Sp.) Sweet, smooth, gentle. Also, **dulcemente.**

dulciana (It.) In organs, a soft stop similar to the diapasons in quality. Also, **echo diapason.**

Dulzian (G.) In organs, an important reed stop. Also, **dulcian.**

dumpf (G.) (1) Dull, hollow, muffled. (2) Depressed, gloomy.

dünn (G.) Thin, tenuous.

duolo, con (It.) Grieving, sorrowful.

dur (1) (F.) Harsh, rough. Also, **avec dureté.** (2) (G.) Major, e.g., *A-dur,* A major.

duramente (It.) Harshly, severely. Also, **duro, con durezza.**

durchsichtig (G.) Transparent, very clear.

durchweg (G.) Consistently, throughout.

duro (It., Sp.) Harsh, rough.

düster (G.) Dark, shadowy, dull.

dynamique (F.) Energetic, vigorous.

E

e (It.) (1) And. (2) Is.

ebbrezza, con (It.) With elation, enraptured, blissful.

eben so (G.) Just as, equally, e.g., *eben so schnell,* just as fast.

éblouissant (F.) Dazzling.

eccitando (It.) Becoming excited or agitated. Also, **eccitato.**

echo (G., etc.) In organs, name for various soft stops, such as **echo diapason, echo dulciana, echo gemshorn,** etc.

écho, en (F.) Echoing.

éclat, avec (F.) With a sudden burst.

éclatant (F.) (1) Brilliant, sparkling. (2) Piercing, shrill.

eco (It.) Echo, an echo effect.

écroulez (F.) Crash down.

ed (It.) And.

effaçant, en s' (F.) Fading away, becoming fainter.

effacé (F.) Suppressed, kept in the background.

effetto, con (It.) Dramatically, forcefully.

effleurant, en (F.) Touching lightly, skimming over.

effleuré (F.) Very light, gliding.

effondrement (F.) Deep-delving.

effusione, con (It.) Pouring out, emotional.

égal (F.) Equal (in duration, time value, etc.). Also, (pl.) **égaux**, e.g., *les triolets égaux*, equal triplets.

également (F.) Uniformly.

eguale (It.) Even, smooth. Also, **egualmente, eguabilmente**.

eigensinnig (G.) Headstrong, unyielding.

eigenwillig (G.) Willful, stubborn.

eilend (G.) Hurrying, rapid. Also, **eilen, mit Eile**.

eilfertig (G.) Hasty, speedy, headlong. Also, **eilig**.

ein (G.) One, a, an. Also, **eine, eins**.

eindringlich (G.) Pressing, urgent.

einfach (G.) (1) Simple, plain. (2) Single (not doubled).

Einleitung (G.) Introduction. Also, **einleiten**, to introduce.

einlenkend (G.) Relenting, yielding.

einmal (G.) Once.

einsetzend (G.) (1) Inserting, interpolating. (2) Installing, establishing.

ein wenig (G.) A little, e.g., *ein wenig schneller*, a little faster.

ekstatisch (G.) Rapturous, ecstatic.

el (Sp.) The.

élan, avec (F.) Bursting out, with dash, vehemently.

élargir (F.) Broaden and slow down. Also, **en élargissant, élargi, elargissez, élargissement**.

elasticito (It.) Springy, bouncy. Also, **con elasticità**.

elastisch (G.) Springy, bouncy, supple.

elegancia, con (Sp.) With elegance, with grace.

elegante (It.) Graceful, polished. Also, **elegantemente, con eleganza**.

elegiaco (It.) Mournful, lamenting.

élégiaque (F.) Mournful.

elevazione, con (It.) Lofty, elevated.

éloignant, en s' (F.) Becoming more distant, fading away. Also, **éloignez**.

eloquenza, con (It.) With eloquence, movingly. Also, **eloquente, eloquentemente**.

emergendo (It.) Becoming distinct, with gradually increasing emphasis. Also, **emergente**.

émouvant (F.) Moving, agitated.

empezar (Sp.) To begin, e.g., *empezar lentamente*, begin slowly.

Empfindung, mit (G.) With feeling, sensitively, tenderly. Also, **empfindsam**.

emphase (F.) Emphasis, stress.

emporté (F.) Fiery, passionate.

empressé (F.) Hurrying, rapid.

ému (F.) With feeling.

en (1) (F.) In. (2) (Sp.) In, at, on, e.g., *en tempo*, in strict time.

encalçando (Port.) Following closely.

enchaînez (F.) Connect, link together, LEGATO. Also, **enchaîner**.

enchantement, en (F.) Entranced, delighted.

encore (F.) Again, once more, still, e.g., *encore plus vite,* still faster.

energico (It.) With vigor, powerfully. Also, **con energia.**

énergique (F.) Vigorous, forceful.

energisch (G.) Same as ÉNERGIQUE.

énervant, en s' (F.) Becoming nervous or irritable, fidgeting.

enfatico (It.) Exaggerated, pompous, with undue emphasis. Also, **con enfasi.**

englisches Horn (G.) English horn.

énigmatique (F.) Mysterious.

enjoué (F.) Cheerful, jovial. Also, **avec enjouement.**

enlevez (F.) Remove, e.g., *enlevez pédal,* remove pedal, *enlevez les sourdines,* remove the mutes.

ensemble (F.) (1) Group of performers. (2) Together.

entêtement, avec (F.) Stubbornly, persistently.

enthousiasme, avec (F.) With enthusiasm, vigorously.

enthusiastisch (G.) Enthusiastic.

entrain, avec (F.) Briskly, with animation, spirited.

entrainant (F.) Eloquently, winningly, captivating.

entrückt (G.) Withdrawn, removed, distant.

entschieden (G.) Determined, decided.

entschlossen (G.) Same as ENTSCHIEDEN.

entusiasmandosi (It.) Enthusiastic, enraptured. Also, **con entusiasmo.**

entusiasmo, con (Sp.) Vigorously, enthusiastically.

Entzücken (G.) Delight. Also, **entzückt,** delighted.

enveloppé (F.) Muffled.

éperdu (F.) Bewildered, distraught.

épouvante surgit, l' (F.) With rising terror.

épuisement (F.) Drained, exhausted.

equilibrado (Sp.) Balanced.

ergeben (G.) (1) To yield. (2) Devoted to, faithful.

ergebungsvoll (G.) Submissive, resigned. Also, **mit Ergebung.**

ergriffen (G.) Deeply moved. Also, **mit Ergriffenheit,** (rarely) **ergreifen.**

erhaben (G.) Lofty, exalted, grand.

erheblich (G.) Considerably, a great deal.

erhoben (G.) Raised, louder, e.g., *mit erhobener Stimme,* in a louder voice.

erlöschend (G.) Fading away.

ermattend (G.) Weakening, becoming softer.

ermunternd (G.) Enlivened, animated.

ernst (G.) Serious, earnest. Also, **ernsthaft.**

ernstlich (G.) Fervent, ardent, with genuine feeling.

eroiccomico (It.) Mock-heroic.

eroico (It.) Heroic, dramatic, melodramatic.

erompente (It.) Bursting forth.

erregt (G.) Excited, agitated, e.g., *mit erregter Stimme,* in an excited tone. Also, **mit Erregung.**

erreichten Tempo, im (G.) Present tempo.

erschöpft (G.) Exhausted.

erschrocken (G.) Startled, frightened.

Erschütterung, mit (G.) Shaken, trembling, with strong feeling.

ersterbend (G.) Fading away.

eruttivo (It.) Eruptive, bursting out.

erzählend (G.) Telling, narrative; sometimes, recitative.

Erzähler (G.) In organs, a foundation stop.

esagerando (It.) Exaggerating, excessive. Also, **esagerato.**

esaltatissimo (It.) Very excited, elated, with great fervor. Also, **con esaltazione.**

esatto (It.) Precise, exact, e.g., *esatto il ritmo,* in precise rhythm, *in tempo esatto,* in exact tempo. Also, **esattamente.**

esitando (It.) Hesitant, wavering. Also, **con esitazione.**

esp. (It.) Short for ESPRESSIVO.

espansivo (It.) Exuberant, broad. Also, **con espansione.**

espirando (It.) (1) Exhaling. (2) Fading away.

espiritu, con (Sp.) With spirit, boldly.

espressivo (It.) With expression, with feeling. Also, **esp., espr., espress., con espressione.**

esquerda (Port.) Left (hand).

estando (It.) Becoming broader, and, usually, louder.

estatico (It.) Rapturous, overwhelmed with joy.

estilo (Sp.) Style.

estinguendosi (It.) Dying away.

estinto (It.) Very soft, barely audible.

estompé (F.) Toned down, muffled.

estremamente (It.) Very, exceedingly. Also, **estremo.**

estribillo (Sp.) Refrain.

esuberante (It.) Lively and loud.

esultante (It.) Rejoicing.

et (F.) And.

éteignant, en s' (F.) Dying away.

éteint (F.) Very soft.

étincelant (F.) Sparkling, brilliant.

étonnement, avec (F.) With astonishment.

étouffé (F.) (1) Damped, i.e., damp sound immediately (in harps, cymbals, etc.). (2) Stifled, choked, muted.

étrange (F.) Strange, odd. Also, **étrangeté,** strangeness.

etwas (G.) Somewhat.

évanouissant, s' (F.) Becoming faint.

évaporant, en (F.) Disappearing.

éveillé (F.) Brisk, animated.

evidente (It.) In evidence, present, audible, e.g., *pianissimo ma evidente,* very soft but audible.

evvivando (It.) Becoming loud, cheering.

ex- (It.) For Italian words, see under *es-*, e.g., for *extatico,* see ESTATICO.

exactamente (Sp.) Strictly.

exagération (F.) Exaggeration.

exaltación, con (Sp.) Exuberant, elevated.

expresivo (Sp.) Same as ESPRESSIVO. Also, **con expresión.**

expressif (F.) Same as ESPRESSIVO.

extasis, con (Sp.) Rapturous.

extatique (F.) Rapturous.

F

f (It.) Short for FORTE.

facile (F., It.) Free, easy, flowing. Also, (F.) **facilement, avec facilité.**

façon, sans (F.) Simply, unaffected.

fagot (Sp.) Bassoon.

Fagott (G.) Bassoon.

fagotto (It.) (1) Bassoon. (2) In organs, an important reed stop.

falsete (Sp.) Falsetto.

falsettirend (G.) In falsetto. Also, **Falsett.**

falsetto (It.) High-pitched and light in quality, like the falsetto voice.

fanatisch (G.) Fanatical, wild.

fanfara (It.) Fanfare.

fantaisie, avec (F.) Freely, capriciously, whimsically. Also, **fantaisiste.**

fantasia, con (It., Sp.) Freely, with imagination.

Fantasieenmässig (G.) See PHANTASIEENMÄSSIG.

fantastico (It.) Fanciful, irregular.

Färbung (G.) Color, tone, e.g., *mit trüber Färbung,* with a dull tone.

farouche (F.) Wild, fierce.

farruco (Sp.) Bold, daring, impudent.

fastidio, con (It.) With annoyance.

fastoso (It.) Pompous, ostentatious.

fausse, faux (F.) False, deceptive.

fausset, en (F.) Head voice, falsetto.

febbrile (It.) Feverish, very excited.

feierlich (G.) Solemn, stately.

Feldflöte (G.) In organs, same as WALDFLÖTE.

felice (It.) Happy, glad, exultant.

feltro (It.(Muffled.

fermamente (It.) Steadily, unwaveringly. Also, **fermo, con fermezza.**

fermata (It.) A pause, usually indicated by the sign ⌢

fermé (F.) Closed. Also, **fermez, fermer.**

fermeté, avec (F.) Firmly, resolutely.

fern (G.) Faraway, distant. Also, **wie aus der Ferne,** as though from a distance.

feroce (It.) Fierce, harsh, wild.

ferre da calza, con (It.) With knitting needles.

fervent (F.) Enthusiastic, devoted.

fervido (It.) Ardent, impassioned.

fervore, con (It.) With vehemence, ardently.

fest (G.) Solid, firm, thorough, e.g., *fest betont,* firmly accented.

festivamente (It.) Joyfully, cheerfully.

festlich (G.) Festive, solemn.

festoso (It.) Merry, gay.

feu, avec (F.) With fire, passionately.

feurig (G.) Fiery, spirited. Also, **mit Feuer.**

ff (It.) Short for FORTISSIMO. Also, **fff.**

fiato (It.) Breath, e.g., *in un sol fiato,* in a single breath, *stromenti di fiato,* wind instruments.

fieberhaft (G.) Excited, restless.

fier, fière (F.) Haughty, bold.

fieramente (It.) Vehemently, boldly. Also, **fiero, con fierezza.**

fièvreux (F.) Feverish, restless, excited.

fila la voce (It.) In vocal music, prolong a note while first swelling and then diminishing in volume.

Filz (G.) Felt (i.e., felt-covered beater).

fin (F., Sp.) End.

fine (It.) End.

finement (F.) Artfully, with skill.

finezza, con (It.) With refinement, elegant.

finster (G.) Dark, somber, sad.

finzione, senza (It.) Open, frank.

fior di labbra, a (It.) See LABBRA, A FIOR DI.

fisarmonica (It.) Accordion.

fisso (It.) Steady, firm.

fitto (It.) Firmly.

Flachflöte (G.) In organs, an open flute stop.

flageolet (F.) (1) An old wind instrument, a type of flute. (2) In organs, an open flute stop. (3) Harmonics.

flageolet harmonique (F.) In organs, an open flute stop.

Flatterzunge (G.) Flutter tonguing.

flauta (Sp.) Flute.

flautada (It.) In organs, a loud, low-pitched foundation stop.

flautando (It.) (1) Flutelike, that is, a light pure tone with few overtones. (2) In bowing, a tone produced by bowing gently but fast over the fingerboard. Also, **flautato.** (3) In stringed instruments (harp, violin, etc.), producing harmonics.

flautín (Sp.) Piccolo.

flautino (It.) (1) Piccolo. (2) Any small flute or recorder. (3) In organs, an open flute stop.

flauto (It.) Flute.

flauto amabile (It.) In organs, same as AMOROSA.

flauto d'amore (It.) In organs, same as FLÛTE D'AMOUR.

flauto dolce (It.) In organs, a very soft open flute stop. Also, **dolce flute, flûte douce.**

flauto mirabilis (It. + L.) In organs, a loud open flute stop with brilliant tone.

flautone (It.) Bass flute.

flauto traverso (It.) (1) Older name for the orchestral flute. (2) In organs, an important open flute stop designed to imitate the tone of the orchestral flute.

flebile (It.) Plaintive, weak, mournful.

flehend (G.) Beseeching, imploring.

flessibile (I.) Agile, flexible.

flicorno (It.) Flugelhorn.

fliessend (G.) Flowing, smooth.

flimmernd (G.) Flickering, wavering.

Flöte (G.) Flute.

Flötenbass (G.) In organs, an open flute stop usually controlled by the pedals. Also, **bass flute, flûte bass.**

flott (G.) Briskly, without hesitation.

flottant (F.) Floating, drifting, irresolute.

flou, floue (F.) Hazy, blurred, indistinct.

flüchtig (G.) Fleeting, skimming over the notes.

fluente (It.) Flowing, pulsating, wave-like.

Flügelhorn (G.) (1) Flugelhorn. (2) In organs, a solo reed stop designed to imitate the tone of the flugelhorn.

fluide (F.) Flowing, smooth.

fluido (It.) Same as FLUIDE.

flüssig (G.) Same as FLUIDE. Also, **mit Fluss.**

flüsternd (G.) Whispering, rustling.

flûte (F.) Flute.

flûte à bec (F.) (1) Recorder. (2) In organs, a soft stop designed to imitate the tone of a recorder.

flûte céleste (F.) In organs, a fairly soft undulating flute stop.

flûte d'amour (F.) In organs, a soft solo flute stop. Also, **flauto d'amore.**

flûte douce (F.) In organs, same as FLAUTO DOLCE.

flutend (G.) Surging, flowing.

flûte ouverte (F.) In organs, an important open flute stop.

flûte triangulaire (F.) In organs, an open flute stop whose pipes are triangular in cross-section.

focosamente (It.) Fiery, ardent, impetuous.

fois (F.) Time(s), e.g., *deux fois,* two times (twice).

fond (F.) Foundation stop.

fond de train, à (F.) At full speed, very fast.

fond doux (F.) A soft foundation stop.

fondu (F.) Becoming softer, dying away.

force, avec (F.) Vigorously, boldly.

fort (F.) (1) Loud. (2) Very, e.g., *fort peu,* very little.

forte (It.) Loud. Also, **f.**

fortepiano (It.) Loud, then soft. Also, **fp.**

fortissimo (It.) Very loud. Also, **ff, fff.**

fortsetzend (G.) Continuing, resuming.

fortwährend (G.) Constant, continuous, incessant.

forza, con (It.) Powerful, forceful, loud.

forzando (It.) A sharp accent. Also, **forzato, fz.**

forzare (It.) To force, to strain, e.g., *forzare la voce,* forcing the voice.

foudroyant (F.) Thundering.

fougueux (F.) Fierce, fiery, spirited.

fourniture (F.) In organs, one of the most important mixture stops.

fp (F.) Short for FORTEPIANO.
fragile (F., It.) Weak, soft.
frais, fraîche (F.) Fresh, brisk.
franchement (F.) Openly, simply, sincerely. Also, **avec franchise.**
frapper (F.) To strike, to pound.
frase (It.) Musical phrase.
fraseggio (It.) Phrasing, articulation.
freddo (It.) Cold, without emotion.
fregando (It.) Rubbing, brushing against, applying friction to.
frei (G.) Free, especially in free tempo.
frei deklamieren (G.) Free recitative.
fremente (It.) (1) Raging, roaring. (2) Quivering, trembling.
frémissant (F.) Trembling.
fremito, come un (It.) (1) Like a roar. (2) Like a tremor.
frenare (It.) To restrain, to hold back.
frenetico (It.) Wild, furious, frenzied.
frénétique (F.) Wild, raving.
freschezza, con (It.) In a fresh, pure style.
frettoloso (It.) Hasty, hurried. Also, **frettoso.**
freudig (G.) Happy, joyful.
freudiger Bewegung, mit (G.) With joyful animation. Also, **mit freudiger Regung.**
freundlich (G.) Friendly, affable.
Frieden, mit (G.) Peacefully, quietly. Also, **friedlich, mit Friedlichkeit.**
frisch (G.) (1) Brisk, gay. Also, **mit Frische.** (2) Fresh, new.

frissonant (F.) Fluttering, trembling.
frivol (G.) Impudent, flippant. Also, **mit Frivolität.**
frivolo (It.) Trifling, frivolous.
froh (G.) Happy.
fröhlich (G.) Joyful.
frohlockend (G.) Jubilant, triumphant.
fromm (G.) Devout, pious.
Frosch, am (G.) At the frog end of the bow.
früher (G.) Earlier, before, e.g., *wie früher,* as before, *früheres Tempo,* (the) previous tempo.
frullato (It.) (1) Hummed, buzzing. (2) Fluttery, agitated.
fruscio (It.) Rustle, murmur. Also, **frusciante.**
fuerte (Sp.) Loud.
fuerza, con (Sp.) Forcefully, loudly.
fugara (It.) In organs, a fairly loud string stop.
fuggevole (It.) Fleeting, rapid. Also, **fuggitivo.**
führend (G.) Leading, uppermost.
fulgurant (F.) Lightning flashes.
funèbre (F.) Funereal, e.g., *marche funèbre,* funeral march.
fúnebre (Sp.) Gloomy, sad.
funereo (It.) Sad, mournful. Also, **funebre.**
fuoco, con (It.) With fire, passionately, excited.
fuori, di (It.) From outside (from backstage).
furioso (It.) Wild, passionate. Also, **con furia.**

furtif, furtive (F.) Stealthy. Also, **furtivement.**

fusa (Sp.) Thirty-second note.

fuso (It.) Joined together, bound.

fuyant (F.) Fleeing, fleeting, fading away.

fz. (It.) Short for FORZANDO.

G

gagliardo (It.) Robust, powerful, vigorous.

gai, gaie (F.) Merry, cheerful. Also, **gaiement, gaîment, avec gaîté (gaieté).**

gaillard (F.) Happy, gay, sprightly.

gaio (It.) Gay, joyful. Also, **con gaiezza.**

gallardía, con (Sp.) Nobly, elegantly.

galoppo, al (It.) At a gallop, very fast.

gamba (It.) (1) Short for viola da gamba, the old bass viol. (2) In organs, an important string stop, with a brilliant, moderately loud tone. Also, (F.) **gambe.**

ganz (G.) Quite, wholly, very, e.g., *ganz langsam,* very slow.

ganze (G.) Whole note (*ganze Note*) or whole rest (*ganze Pause*).

garbato (It.) Graceful, elegant. Also, (It., Sp.) **con garbo.**

gavotta (It.) Gavotte.

gebunden (G.) Smooth, tied, LEGATO.

Gedackt (G.) In organs, an important stopped flute pipe. Also, **Gedeckt.**

gedämpft (G.) Muted, muffled.

Gedeckt (G.) Same as GEDACKT.

Gedecktpommer (G.) In organs, a stopped flute stop. Also, **Pommer.**

gedehnt (G.) Dragging, slow.

gedrängt (G.) Compact, compressed, faster.

gefasst (G.) Calm, tranquil, resigned.

gefühlvoll (G.) With feeling, tenderly. Also, **mit Gefühl.**

gehalten (G.) Held, sustained.

geheimnisvoll (G.) Mysterious.

gehend (G.) Moving at a moderate tempo, same as ANDANTE. Also, **gehender.**

gehetzt (G.) Driven.

Geige (G.) Violin.

Geigenbass (G.) In organs, a low-pitched foundation stop of diapason tone.

gekichert (G.) Giggled, tittered.

gekoppelt (G.) Coupled.

gelassen (G.) Quiet, calm, unhurried.

geläufig (G.) Flowing, smooth.

gélido (Sp.) Icy, frigid.

gelöster (G.) Looser, freer.

gemach (G.) Softly and gently, gradually.

gemächlich (G.) Comfortable, leisurely.

gemässigt (G.) Moderate.

gemendo (It.) Lamenting.

gemessen (G.) At a regular pace, in steady rhythm.

gemischt (G.) Mixed, e.g., *gemischte Stimmen,* mixed voices.

Gemshorn (G.) In organs, an important foundation stop.

gemütlich (G.) Comfortable, leisurely.

gentilmente (It.) Gently, with refinement.

gentiment (F.) Prettily, daintily.

gepresst (G.) (1) Crowded, overfull. (2) In vocal music, in a choked voice. (3) Depressed, dejected.

gering, geringer, geringes (G.) Little, smaller.

gerissen (G.) (1) Dragged, pulled along. (2) Cunning, sly.

gerührt (G.) To feel moved or deeply touched.

gesammelt (G.) Gathered together.

Gesang (G.) Singing, voice, vocal part.

gesanglich (G.) Vocal part.

gesangvoll (G.) Songlike. Also, **gesangartig, gesangreich**.

gesättigt (G.) Satisfied, full, e.g., *mit gesättigtem Ton,* with a full tone.

geschäftig (G.) Bustling, stirring.

geschlagen (G.) Struck, e.g., *mit dem Bogen geschlagen,* hitting the bow (against the strings).

geschleift (G.) Slurred, bound, LEGATO.

geschlossen (G.) Closed.

geschmeidig (G.) Flexible, agile, glib, e.g., *mit geschmeidiger Bewegung,* with flexible movement, with agility.

geschwind (G.) Quick, nimble.

gespannt (G.) (1) Restless, expectant, tense. (2) Drawn out.

gespenstig (G.) Ghostly. Also, **gespentisch**.

gesperrt (G.) Spaced out, spread.

gesprochen (G.) Spoken.

gesteigert (G.) Increased, intensified, louder.

gestopft (G.) Stopped (in horns).

gestossen (G.) Abrupt, disconnected, STACCATO.

gestrafft (G.) Tight, tense, concise.

gestrichen (G.) (1) Bowed. (2) Passing over softly and smoothly, LEGATO. (3) In notation, describing notes above or below the staff, which require ledger lines.

gesummt (G.) Hummed.

gesungen (G.) Sung.

geteilt (G.) Same as DIVISI; *nicht geteilt,* not divisi (i.e., UNISONO).

getragen (G.) Sustained and slow, same as SOSTENUTO.

gettato (It.) Same as JETÉ. Also, **gettate**.

gewichtig (G.) Weighty, pompous.

gewissen (G.) (1) Particular, certain, e.g., *mit einem gewissen Schwung,* with a certain lilt. (2) Conscience, e.g., *ein gutes Gewissen,* a clear conscience.

gewöhnlich (G.) Ordinary, as usual, simple.

gezogen (G.) Drawn out, sustained.

giocondamente (It.) Joyfully, happily. Also, **giocondo**.

giocoso (It.) Jocose, humorous. Also, **giuocando, con gioco**.

gioioso (It.) Joyous, cheerful. Also, **con gioia**.

Gitarre (G.) Guitar.

giubilando (It.) Rejoicing, exultant. Also, **giubilante, giubiloso, con giubilo.**

giudaïco, in modo (It.) In the Jewish manner (like Jewish chant).

giulivo (It.) Merry, festive, joyful.

giuocando (It.) Same as GIOCOSO.

giusto (It.) Just, right, appropriate, e.g., *tempo giusto,* appropriate tempo (or strict tempo).

glänzend (G.) Brilliant, splendid. Also, **glanzvoll.**

glas, comme un (F.) Like a death knell.

glashart (G.) Clear, crystalline, brilliant.

gleich (G.) (1) The same. Also, **gleiches, gleicher.** (2) Immediately, at once.

gleichförmig (G.) Equal, uniform, even.

gleichgültig (G.) Careless, casual, indifferent.

gleichmässig (G.) Even, regular.

gleitend (G.) Gliding, smooth.

gli (It.) The.

glissando (pseud. It.) A glide from one note to the next. Also, **gliss.**

glissez (F.) Slide (over the notes), a GLISSANDO.

glitzernd (G.) Sparkling.

Glocke (G.) Bell.

Glockenspiel (G.) In organs, same as CARILLON (2).

glorioso (It.) Glorious, splendid.

glühend (G.) Glowing, ablaze, fervent.

goffaggine, con una (It.) Awkwardly, clumsily. Also, **goffamente.**

Gong (G.) Gong.

gosier, dans le (F.) In the throat.

goutte, une (F.) A drop, like a raindrop.

gracia, con (Sp.) Graceful. Also, **gracioso, graciosamente.**

gracieux, gracieuse (F.) Graceful, elegant. Also, **gracieusement, avec grâce.**

gracile (It.) Delicate, graceful.

gracioso (Sp.) (1) Graceful, refined. (2) Witty, humorous. (3) Jester, clown.

gradatamente (It.) Gradually, step by step.

gradazione, con (It.) By degrees, subtly shading.

gradevole (It.) Pleasant, pleasing. Also, **gradevolmente.**

grado a grado la corda (It.) Scale step by scale step on the string.

gran cassa (It.) Bass drum. Also, **gran tamburo.**

grand bourdon (F.) In organs, a special mixture stop made up of several ranks of stopped flute pipes.

grand-choeur (F.) Full organ.

grand détaché (F.) In bowing, alternate up- and down-bows, but with long strokes. (See also DÉTACHÉ.)

grande (It.) Broadly.

grandendo (It.) Becoming broader.

grandezza, con (It.) With grandeur, stately. Also, (It., Sp.) **grandioso.**

grand-orgue (F.) Great organ. Also, G^d-o.

grave (F., It.) (1) Flat, low-pitched. (2) Solemn, serious, slow. Also, (F.) **gravement, avec gravité**, (It.) **gravemente, con gravità**.

gravissima (It.) In organs, a very low-pitched bass stop on the pedals. Also, **acoustic bass, resultant, vox gravissima**.

gravità, con (It.) Dignified, serious.

gravitätisch (G.) Grave, solemn.

grazio, con (It.) With grace, prettily.

graziös (G.) Graceful.

grazioso (It.) Graceful and easy, ANDANTE.

grell (G.) Shrill, strident.

grida (It.) Proclamation.

gridando (It.) Shouting. Also, **gridato**.

Griffbrett, am (G.) On the fingerboard. Also, **auf dem Griffbrett**.

grimmig (G.) Fierce, raging, vehement, intense.

grive musicienne (F.) Song thrush.

grollend (G.) Angry, sullen.

gros, grosse (F.) Rough, loud, massive.

gross, grosse, grosser (G.) Large.

grosse caisse (F.) Bass drum.

Grosse Trommel (G.) Bass drum.

Grossflöte (G.) In organs, an 8-foot open flute stop on both manuals and pedals.

grossièrement (F.) Roughly.

grossissant la voix, en (F.) Swelling, becoming louder and louder.

grossolano (It.) Rough, coarse, crude.

grotesk (G.) Fantastic, grotesque.

grottescamente (It.) Grotesquely, fancifully. Also, **grottesco**.

Grundeinheit (G.) Basic unit, basic meter.

Grundtempo (G.) Basic tempo.

gruppo (It.) A turn. Also, **gruppetto**.

guajira (Sp.) (1) A type of Cuban popular song. (2) Rustic, boorish.

guerra, alla (It.) In a martial style.

guilleret (F.) Lively, brisk.

guitare (F.) Guitar.

guitarra (Sp.) Guitar.

gusto, con (It.) With style, with zest.

gut (G.) Well, thoroughly, e.g., *gut rhythmisiert*, thoroughly rhythmic.

H

habanera (Sp.) A Cuban dance with distinctive rhythm.

habgierig (G.) Greedy, grasping.

haché (F.) Choppy, abrupt, irregular.

halb (G.) Half, e.g., *halb gesungen*, half sung.

Halbe (G.) Half note (*Halbe Note*) or half rest (*Halbe Pause*).

Halbton (G.) Half tone, semitone.

haletant (F.) Panting, gasping.

Harfe (G.) Harp.

Harfenprinzipal (G.) In organs, a soft diapason stop.

harmonia aetheria (L.) In organs, a soft manual mixture stop.

Harmonie (G.) Harmony, chords.

harmonieux (F.) Melodious.

Harmonika (G.) In organs, an 8-foot manual open flute stop. Also, **harmonica.**

harpe (F.) Harp.

hart (G.) Hard, firm, solid.

Hartfilz (G.) A hard felt beater (for drums).

hasta (Sp.) Up to, until, e.g., *hasta la extinción del sonido*, until the sound ceases.

hastig (G.) (1) With haste, hurrying. Also, **hastend.** (2) Abruptly, suddenly.

hâte, sans (F.) Without haste, easily, deliberately. Also, **ne hâtez pas.**

Hauch, wie ein (G.) Like a breath, very lightly.

Hauptzeitmass (G.) Main tempo.

hautbois (F.) (1) Oboe. (2) In organs, an 8-foot manual reed stop designed to sound like the orchestral oboe.

hautbois d'amour (F.) Same as OBOE D'AMORE.

heftig (G.) (1) Violent, strong. (2) Very, e.g., *heftig bewegt*, very lively.

heilig (G.) Holy, sacred.

heimlich (G.) Secretly, stealthily.

heiser (G.) Hoarse, e.g., *mit heiserer Stimme*, with a hoarse voice.

heiter (G.) Cheerful, gay.

heldenhaft (G.) Heroically, in a stalwart manner.

hell (G.) Clear, ringing.

Hellflöte (G.) In organs, an open flute stop with a loud, bright tone.

herantrippelnd (G.) Tripping along.

herausheben (G.) Emphasize, set off (from the background).

héroïque (F.) Noble, grand.

herrisch (G.) Overbearing, haughty.

Herunterstrich (G.) Down-bow.

hervor (G.) Forward, bring out, emphasize. Also, **hervorheben.**

hervorbrechend (G.) Bursting out.

hervorgehoben (G.) Emphasized, accented.

hervortretend (G.) Standing out, emphasized.

herzlich (G.) Hearty, warm, sincere.

hésitant (F.) Wavering, hanging back.

heurté (F.) Abrupt, harsh, jerky.

Hinaufstrich (G.) Up-bow. Also, **Hinstrich.**

Hingebung, mit (G.) Enthusiastically, faithfully. Also, **hingebend.**

hingeworfen (G.) Quick, flighty.

hinhaltend (G.) Holding back, delaying.

hinsterbend (G.) Fading away.

hinströmend (G.) Flowing.

hintersinnig (G.) Melancholy, sad.

hoch (G.) High, upward, e.g., *Stürzen hoch*, bells up.

Höhepunkt (G.) Climax.

hohl (G.) Hollow, dull, muffled.

Hohlflöte (G.) In organs, an open flute stop. Also, **Hohlpfeife.**

höhnisch (G.) Derisive, mocking, scornful. Also, **höhnend.**

Holzrankett (G.) In organs, a rankett stop with wooden (instead of metal) resonators.

Holzregal (G.) In organs, a wooden reed stop.

hörbar (G.) Audible.

Horn (G.) Usually, French horn. Sometimes, saxhorn. Also, **Hörner** (pl.).

huitième de soupir (F.) Thirty-second rest.

humeur, avec (F.) With humor, fanciful.

Humor, mit (G.) With humor, facetiously. Also, **humorvoll**.

humoristico (Sp.) Jovial, amiable.

hurtig (G.) Rapid, agile.

huschend (G.) Scurrying, gliding by.

hymnenartig (G.) Hymnlike. Also, **hymnisch**.

I

i (It.) The.

I° (It.) Short for primo (see PRIMA).

idyllisch (G.) Idyllic, pastoral.

ieratico (It.) Solemn, stylized.

igual (Sp.) Even, uniform.

il (It.) The.

im (G.) In the.

imitando (It.) Imitating, echoing.

immer (G.) Always, constantly, e.g., *immer gleiches Zeitmass,* always in the same tempo.

immobile (It.) Motionless.

impavido (It.) Fearless, undaunted.

imperceptible (Sp.) Very soft, scarcely audible.

impérieux (F.) Commanding, haughty.

imperioso (It., Sp.) Stately, dignified, commanding.

impeto, con (It.) With violence, rushing in.

impétueux (F.) Impetuous, vehement, headlong. Also, **impétueusement**.

impetuoso (It.) Violent, impetuous.

implacable (F.) Unyielding, unrelenting, constant, e.g., *presto implacable,* constantly very fast.

implorant (F.) Beseeching.

improvisando (It.) Improvising.

improvisant, en (F.) Same as IMPROVISANDO.

improvisation, comme une (F.) As though improvised.

inbrünstig (G.) Ardent, passionate.

incalzando (It.) Pressing on, hurrying.

incamminando (It.) Setting forth, initiating.

incantando (It.) Enchanting, delighting.

incisif (F.) Sharp, precise.

incisivo (It.) Incisive, clear-cut, sharply delineated. Also, **inciso**.

incolore (F., It.) Steady, without color or emphasis.

incubo, come in (It.) As in a nightmare.

indécis (F.) Hesitant, wavering.

indifférent (F.) Without emotion.

indifferente (It.) Apathetic.

indistinto (It.) Blurred, vague, faint.

indolemment (F.) Lazily.

indolente (It.) Listless, apathetic.

in due (It.) (1) In two parts (voice-parts). (2) With two beats.

indugiando (It.) Delaying, retarding.

inflessione (It.) (1) Inflection, e.g., *inflessione di voce*, vocal inflection, *senza inflessioni*, without inflections. (2) Flexibility, e.g., *inflessione di tempo*, a flexible tempo, not too strict.

inflexible (F.) Firm, decisive, unwavering.

infuorandosi (It.) Becoming enraged. Also, **infuriando.**

ingenuità, con (It.) Innocently, simply, sincerely.

ingénuo (Sp.) Open, candid, artless. Also, (Port.) **ingênuo**, (Sp.) **ingenuamente.**

iniziale (It.) Original, e.g., *tempo iniziale*, original tempo. Also, **inizio** (*tempo d'inizio*).

inner, innere, inneres (G.) Inner, interior, e.g., *innere Stimme*, inner voice-part.

innig (G.) Heartfelt, tender.

innocemment (F.) Simple, artless.

innodia, coma una (It.) Hymnlike.

inocente (Sp.) Simple, plain.

inquiet (F.) Uneasy, agitated.

inquieto (It.) Restless, uneasy.

insensibilmente (It.) Very slightly, scarcely at all.

inserirsi (It.) Inserted, interpolated.

insidioso (It.) Treacherously, insidiously, insinuated.

insinuante (It.) Suggested.

insistenza, con (It.) Obstinate, persistent. Also, **insistendo.**

inspirant, en (F.) Inhaling.

intensiv (G.) Intense, ardent, vehement.

intensificando (It.) Intensifying, becoming louder.

intenso (It.) Intense, violent. Also, **intensito, intensamente, con intensità.**

intenzionato (It.) Amiable, willing.

intenzione, con (It.) Purposeful, deliberate.

intimement (F.) Intimately, confidentially, quietly.

intimo (It., Sp.) Intimately, familiar.

intrepido (It.) Fearless, undaunted, bold.

invocando (It.) Calling upon.

irato (It.) Furious, enraged.

irisé (F.) Iridescent, shimmering.

ironico (It.) Ironical.

ironique (F.) Mocking.

irrationnel (F.) Unequal.

irréel (F.) Imaginary, fanciful, otherworldly. Also, **irréelment.**

irrequieto (It.) Restless, uneasy.

irresoluto (It.) Uncertain, tentative.

irritant, en s' (F.) Becoming angry.

irritato (It.) Provoked, annoyed.

islancio, con (It.) With dash, with verve.

isoritmico (It.) Isorhythmic, i.e., repeating a fixed rhythmic pattern.

istesso tempo, l' (It.) At the same tempo. Also, **lo stesso tempo.**

izquierdo (Sp.) Left (hand).

J

j For Italian words, see under *gi-*, e.g., for *jubilo*, see GIUBILO.

jauchzend (G.) Shouting with joy, exultant, cheering.

jede, jeder, jedes (G.) Every, any.

jedesmal (G.) Every time, always.

jedoch (G.) Yet, still, nevertheless.

jeté (F.) Throwing the bow against the string so that it will rebound several times on the down-bow.

jeu (F.) Organ stop.

jeu de clochette (F.) In organs, a manual mixture stop.

jeux doux (F.) Soft organ stops.

jeux forts (F.) Loud organ stops.

jocoso (Sp.) Humorous.

joyeux (F.) Happy, lighthearted. Also, **joyeusement.**

Jubalflöte (G.) In organs, same as SERAPHONFLÖTE.

jubelnd (G.) Rejoicing, exulting. Also, **jubilierend.**

juego de timbres (Sp.) Glockenspiel. Also, **órgano de campanas.**

jünglingshaften (G.) Youthful.

juntos (Sp.) Together.

jusqu'à (F.) Up to, e.g., *jusqu'à la fin,* up to the end.

K

Kadenz (G.) (1) Cadence. (2) Cadenza.

kadenzartig (G.) Like a cadenza.

kapriziös (G.) Willful, capricious, whimsical.

karikiert (G.) Caricatured.

kaum (G.) Scarcely, hardly, e.g., *kaum betont,* scarcely accented, *kaum hörbar,* scarcely audible.

keck (G.) Bold, impudent.

keifend (G.) Scolding, jangling, yelping.

kein, keine, keiner (G.) No, none, e.g., *keine Betonung,* no accent.

klagend (G.) Lamenting, plaintive. Also, **kläglich.**

Klang (G.) Sound.

klangvoll (G.) Ringing, resounding.

Klappe (G.) Key or valve (in wind instruments.)

klar (G.) Clear, distinct.

Klarinette (G.) Clarinet.

Klavier (G.) Piano.

kleine Mixture (G.) In organs, a soft manual mixture stop.

Kleinerzähler (G.) In organs, a 4-foot manual foundation stop.

Kleinflöte (G.) In organs, a 4-foot manual flute stop.

Kleinprinzipal (G.) In organs, a 4-foot foundation stop on the manuals.

klingen lassen (G.) Let sound.

klingt (G.) Rings, sounds.

Knopfregal (G.) In organs, a reed stop of the regal group.

kokett (G.) Flirtatious.

Kontrabass (G.) Double bass, contrabass.

Kontrafagott (G.) Contrabassoon.

Koppel (G.) Coupler.

Koppelflöte (G.) In organs, an open flute stop.

Kornett (G.) Cornet.

kosend (G.) Caressingly, fondly.

Kraft, mit (G.) Vigorously, forcefully. Also, **kräftig, kraftvoll.**

kreischend (G.) Strident, shrill.

Krummhorn (G.) (1) Crumhorn (obsolete woodwind). (2) In organs, an 8-foot solo reed stop on the manuals. Also, (F., It.) **cromorne.**

kurz, kurze, kurzer (G.) Short, brief, e.g., *kurzer Halt,* short pause.

L

l' (F.) The.

la (F., It., Sp.) The.

labbra (It.) Lip.

labbra, a fior di (It.) At the front of the mouth, i.e., very lightly and softly sung or spoken.

lacerante (It.) Tearing, rending.

lâchez (F.) Release.

lacrimoso (It.) Mournful, tearful. Also, **lagrimoso.**

Lage (G.) Position (in playing violins, etc.).

lagnoso (It.) Lamenting, miserable.

lagrimoso (Sp.) Same as LACRIMOSO.

laissez (F.) (1) Depart, leave, leave alone. (2) Let, e.g., *laissez vibrer,* let sound (or release damper).

lamento, con (It.) Mournful, plaintive. Also, **lamentevole, lamentoso.**

lancer (F.) To launch, to begin, e.g., *lancer le mouvement,* to launch a (new) tempo.

lancio, con (It.) With verve, flinging.

Ländler (G.) A dance similar to a slow waltz.

lang, lange, langer (G.) Long, long-lasting, e.g., *lange Pause,* long rest.

langsam (G.) Slow. Also, **langsamer,** slower.

languendo (It.) Weak, faint, languishing. Also, **languido.**

languidez (Port.) Languor, listlessness, weakness.

languissament (F.) Languishing. Also, **languissante.**

largamente (It.) Broadly.

largando (It.) Becoming broader, slowing down.

large (F.) Broad, full, fairly slow. Also, **largement.**

larghetto (It.) A slow tempo, not quite as slow as LARGO.

largo (It.) Slow, solemn, sustained, a tempo slower than LENTO but not as slow as GRAVE.

larigot (F.) In organs, a foundation rank of diapason pipes which sound two octaves and one fifth higher than the keys played. Also, **nineteenth.**

las (Sp.) The.

las, lasse (F.) Tired, weary. Also, **lassé.**

lasciare (It.) To let, to allow, e.g., *lasciare vibrare,* let sound (continue to sound).

lassen (G.) To let, to allow, e.g., *vibrieren lassen,* let sound (continue to sound).

lässig (G.) Slow, lackadaisical.

lastend (G.) Weighty, ponderous.

Laune, mit (G.) (1) In a good humor. (2) Ill-tempered, peevish.

launig (G.) Humorous, droll.

launisch (G.) Moody, capricious, changeable, ill-tempered.

laut (G.) Loud.

Laute (G.) Lute.

lauter (G.) Louder.

le (F., It.) The.

lebendig (G.) Lively.

lebhaft (G.) Animated, lively.

légal (F.) Strict, e.g., *mouvement légal*, strict tempo.

legato (It.) Smooth, even, without any break between notes. Also, **leg.**

légendaire (F.) Legendary.

léger (F.) Light, quick. Also, **légèrement.**

leggerezza, con (It.) Lightly, nimbly. Also, **leggero, leggiero.**

leggiadro (It.) Graceful, elegant, light.

legni (It.) The woodwind section.

legno, col (It.) Playing with the wood (stick) of the bow by bouncing it against the strings.

legnoso (It.) Stiff, wooden.

leicht (G.) Light.

leichthin (G.) Light, airy, flippant.

leidenschaftlich (G.) Passionately. Also, **mit Leidenschaft.**

leiernd (G.) Droning, monotonous.

leise (G.) Soft.

lejanía, como en (Sp.) As if from a distance, faraway.

lejano (Sp.) Distant, soft.

lent (F.) Slow. Also, **lentement, avec lenteur.**

lentamente (It.) Slowly.

lento (It., Sp.) A slow tempo.

lento epico (It.) Slow and stately.

les (F.) The.

letargico (It.) Torpid, lethargic.

leuchtend (G.) Glowing, luminous, brilliant.

levare (It.) To take off (organ stops, mutes). Also, **levate, si levano.**

leve (Sp., Port.) Light. Also, (Port.) **com leveza.**

lezioso (It.) Affected, mincing. Also, **leziosamente.**

L.H. (G.) Short for left hand.

libero (It.) Freely. Also, **liberamente.**

libre (F.) Free, unrestrained. Also, **librement.**

libro aperto, a (It.) At sight, sight-reading.

licenza, con (It.) Freely, at the performer's discretion.

lié (F.) Tied, bound, LEGATO.

liebenswürdig (G.) Amiable, pleasant, charming.

lieblich (G.) Lovely, sweet, melodious.

liegen lassen (G.) Keep down, e.g., *Pedal liegen lassen*, keep pedal depressed.

lieto (It.) Gay, joyful.

lieve (It.) Light, easy. Also, **lievemente.**

ligado (Sp.) (1) Same as LEGATO. (2) Ligature.

ligar (Sp.) To tie together, to bind.

ligero (Sp.) Light, rapid.

limpide (F.) Clear, transparent.

linke Hand (G.) Left hand. Also, **L.H.**

lirico (It.) (1) Pertaining to opera, e.g., *artista lirico,* opera singer. (2) Lyrical, poetic.

lírico (Sp.) Lyrical, songlike. Also, **con lirismo.**

liscio (It.) Smooth, even, regular.

lispelnd (G.) Lisping, whispering, murmuring.

lisse (F.) Smooth, polished.

liuto (It.) Lute.

liviano (Sp.) Light, fleeting, frivolous.

lleno (Sp.) In organs, a mixture stop.

lo (It.) The.

lo, los (Sp.) The.

locker (G.) Loose, gay, easy.

loco (It.) Return to normal position (after OTTAVA).

loin (F.) Distant, soft. Also, **lointain.**

lontanando (It.) Fading into the distance.

lontano (It.) Far-off, remote. Also, **come in lontananza,** as if from a distance.

losbrechen (G.) Burst out, break forth. Also, **losbrechend.**

lourd (F.) Weighty, strong. Also, **lourdement, avec lourdeur.**

louré (F.) (1) In bowing, a LEGATO but with emphasis on each note. (2) Sounding continuously, like a bagpipe drone.

lucide (F.) Clear, limpid.

luftig (G.) Light, airy.

Luftpause (G.) Pause for breath, either literally or figuratively.

lugubre (1) (It.) Dismal, dark, sad. (2) (F.) Mournful.

luisant (F.) Glittering, shimmering.

lumineux (F.) Clear, luminous.

luminoso (It.) Bright, shining, clear.

lunga, lungo (It.) Long, sustained, e.g., *lunga pausa,* rest, fermata.

lusingando (It.) Caressing, alluring.

lusinghiero (It.) Flattering, pleasing, caressing.

lustig (G.) Merry, cheerful.

luttuoso (It.) Doleful, sad.

lyrique (F.) Sweetly singing, melodious.

lyrisch (G.) Same as LYRIQUE.

M

ma (It.) But, e.g., *piano ma ben marcato,* soft but well accented.

mächtig (G.) (1) Powerful, loud. (2) Very, considerably, e.g., *mächtig bewegt,* quite lively.

maestoso (It.) With dignity, nobly. Also, **con maestà.**

maggiore (It.) Major.

magico (It.) Magical, enchanting.

main droite (F.) Right hand. Also, **m.d.**

main gauche (F.) Left hand. Also, **m.g.**

mais (F.) But.

majestätisch (G.) Stately.

majestueux (F.) Stately, majestic. Also, **majestueusement, avec majesté.**

majestuoso (Sp.) Same as MAESTOSO.

malice, avec (F.) Spitefully, slyly, mischievously.

malinconico (It.) Melancholy, gloomy. Also, **malinconia**.

malizioso (It.) Cunning, malicious, mischievous. Also, **con malizia**.

mancando (It.) Becoming softer, fading.

mano (It., Sp.) Hand.

marc. (It.) Short for MARCATO.

marcado (Port., Sp.) Marked, pronounced, same as MARCATO.

marcata (It.) Mark, emphasize, e.g., *marcata il basso,* emphasize the bass (part), *marcata la melodia* (*il canto*), emphasize the melody.

marcato (It.) Accented, stressed. Also, **marcando, marc.**

marche (F.) March.

märchenhaft (G.) Fairylike, fanciful.

marcia (It.) March, e.g., *alla marcia funebre,* like a funeral march, *alla marcia,* in march time.

marciale (It.) Marchlike, martial.

markiert (G.) Accented, same as MARCATO.

markig (G.) Vigorous.

marqué (F.) Marked, accented, emphasized, same as MARCATO. Also, **marquez**, emphasize, e.g., *marquez le chant,* emphasize the melody.

marschmässig (G.) In march style.

Marschzeitmass (G.) March tempo.

martelé (F.) (1) In bowing, heavy, detached up-and-down strokes, played by releasing each bow stroke suddenly, and using the point of the bow. (2) In piano playing, etc., a forceful, detached effect, created by releasing the keys suddenly.

martellato (It.) Same as MARTELÉ.

marziale (It.) Martial, military.

mas (Sp.) But.

más (Sp.) More, most, e.g., *a más correr,* as fast as possible.

más bien (Sp.) Rather, quite.

maschio (It.) Manly.

más que (Sp.) More than, but only, even if.

massiccio (It.) Solid, heavy.

mässig (G.) (1) Moderately, e.g., *mässig bewegt,* moderately lively. (2) A moderate tempo, same as MODERATO.

matices, sin (Sp.) Without shading, without emphasis. Also, **sin matiz**.

maxixando (Port.) Like a maxixe (the Brazilian dance).

m.d. (F., It.) Right hand.

meccanico (It.) Mechanical, without expressing emotion.

méchamment (F.) Spitefully, mischievously.

méchant (F.) Wicked, malicious.

medesimo (It.) The same, e.g., *al medesimo tempo,* at the same tempo.

media (Sp.) Moderate, e.g., *a media fuerza,* with moderate loudness.

media vozi, a (Sp.) Half-voice.

medio fuerte (Sp.) Moderately loud.

medir (Sp.) Measure, meter.

meditabondo (It.) Thoughtful, reflective. Also, **meditando**.

mehr (G.) More.

melancholisch (G.) Sad.

melancólico (Sp.) Sad, gloomy. Also, **melancolía**.

mélancolique (F.) Sad, mournful, plaintive.

melodia (It.) Melody.

melodico (It.) Melodic, tuneful.

Melodie (G.) Melody.

mélodique (F.) Melodious, tuneful, songlike. Also, **mélodieux**.

mélopée (F.) Chant, intonation, recitative.

même (F.) Same.

menaçant (F.) Threatening, foreboding.

meno (It.) Less, e.g., *meno andante*, less slow (faster), *meno piano*, less soft (louder), *meno mosso (motto)*, less movement (slower).

menos (Sp.) Less, least.

Menschenstimme (G.) In organs, same as VOX HUMANA.

meravigliato (It.) Astonished, amazed.

mesto (It.) Sad, mournful. Also, **mestamente**.

mesure (F.) (1) Measure, bar. (2) Time, meter.

mesuré (F.) (1) In strict time. Also, **en mesure**. (2) Measured, deliberate, moderate.

metà, la (It.) Half.

metallico (It.) Metallic, with a tinny sound.

metallo (It.) Vocal timbre, tone.

metà strada, a (It.) Halfway between.

mètre de Maelzel (F.) Referring to the beat marked by a Maelzel metronome.

metrum (L.) Meter.

mettez (F.) Put, place, use; in organ music, to draw a stop. Also, **mettez les sourdines,** use the mutes.

mezzo, mezza (It.) Medium, half, e.g., *mezzo forte* (*mf*), moderately loud, softer than forte, *mezzo piano* (*mp*), moderately soft, louder than piano but less loud than mezzo forte, *mezza voce,* half voice.

mf (It.) Short for MEZZO forte.

m.g. (F.) Left hand.

minaccioso (It.) Threatening, menacing.

minore (It.) Minor.

mismo (Sp.) Same.

misterioso (It.) Mysterious, secretive.

mistico (It.) Mystical, spiritual.

misura (It.) Meter, beat, e.g., *senza misura,* not in strict time, *alla (con) misura,* in strict time, *misura binaria,* duple meter.

misurato (It.) Measured, moderate, in strict time.

mit (G.) With.

mite (It.) Gentle, moderate.

mi-voix, à (F.) Half-voice, softly, in an undertone.

mobile (It.) Changeable, capricious.

mod. (It.) Short for MODERATO.

moderado (Sp.) A moderate tempo, MODERATO.

moderato (It.) A moderate tempo, neither fast nor slow.

modéré (F.) At a moderate tempo. Also, **modérément.**

modificazioni, senza (It.) Without changes, as written.

modo (It.) Manner, style, e.g., *in modo ordinario,* in the ordinary (customary) manner, *in modo di ballo,* in dance style.

modo de, a (Sp.) In the style of.

moëlleux (F.) Soft, mellow.

möglich (G.) Possible, e.g., *so laut als möglich,* as loud as possible.

moins (F.) Less.

moins, au (F.) At least.

moins encore (F.) Still less.

moins que (F.) Less than.

moitié (F.) Half.

moll (G.) Minor, e.g., *A-moll,* A minor.

molle (It.) Soft, languid. Also, **mollemente.**

mollezza, con (It.) Delicately.

molto (It.) Very, much, e.g., *molto allegro,* very fast.

momentaneamente (It.) Momentarily.

monotamente (It.) Very evenly, without much expression.

monoton (G.) Monotonous, droning.

monotone (F.) Monotonous, very even.

monotonía, con (Sp.) Monotonously. Also, **monótono.**

montant (F.) Becoming louder.

montre (F.) In organs, a name for visible principal pipes that actually sound (rather than designed merely for appearance).

moqueur (F.) Jeering, deriding.

morbido (It.) Soft, delicate.

morboso (It.) Morbid.

mordant (F.) Biting, sharp.

mordente (It.) (1) Biting, pungent. (2) An ornament (the mordent).

morendo (It.) Fading away.

mormorando (It.) Murmuring, whispering. Also, **mormorato, come un mormorio.**

morne (F.) Gloomy, sad.

mosso (It.) Moved, agitated, e.g., *più mosso,* more moved (faster), *meno mosso,* slower.

moto, con (It.) Somewhat lively, not too slowly. Also, *andante con moto,* moderately slow but not too slow.

mourant, en (F.) Dying away, becoming faint.

mouvement (F.) (1) Tempo, e.g., *mouvement du début,* original tempo, *au mouvement,* in tempo. (2) Section (movement) of a sonata, symphony, etc.

mouvementé (F.) Lively, animated.

mouvement légal (F.) Strict tempo.

movendo (It.) Moving along.

movido (Sp.) Moving along, rapid.

movimento (It.) Tempo, e.g., *lo stesso movimento,* the same tempo.

movimiento (Sp.) (1) Tempo, time. (2) Motion, movement.

moyen, moyenne (F.) Average, medium, moderate.

mp (It.) Short for MEZZO piano.

mucho (Sp.) Much, a great deal, very.

müde (G.) Weary, exhausted. Also, **Müdigkeit**.

muet, muette (F.) Silent, mute.

muito (Port.) Much, a great deal, very.

mujer (Sp.) Female, e.g., *mujer voz*, female voice.

Mund (G.) Mouth.

munter (G.) Cheerful, merry.

muovere un poco (It.) Keep going, keep moving.

murmuré (F.) Murmured, whispered. Also, **comme un murmure**.

musette (F.) (1) Bagpipe. (2) In organs, a moderately soft solo reed stop.

muta (It.) In timpani parts, indication for change of tuning.

mutamento (It.) Change, alteration, e.g., *senza mutamenti una corda*, without releasing the una corda (soft) pedal.

mutazione, registro di (It.) Mutation stop.

mutig (G.) Courageous, bold.

muy (Sp.) Very, much, e.g., *muy sentido*, very eloquent.

mystérieux (F.) Mysterious. Also, **mystérieusement**.

mystique (F.) Mystical, otherworldly, ethereal.

mystisch (G.) Mystical.

N

nach (G.) (1) After. (2) Behind. (3) In the manner of, according to, e.g., *nach Bedürfniss*, according to the performer's discretion.

nachdenklich (G.) Thoughtful, meditative.

Nachdruck, mit (G.) Emphatically, firmly, vigorously. Also, **nachdrücklich**.

nachgeben (G.) Give way, slacken.

nachlassend (G.) Slackening, slowing down and/or diminishing.

Nachschlag (G.) Ornament ending a trill, e.g., *ohne Nachschlag*, a trill perfomed without the concluding ornament.

Nachthorn (G.) In organs, an important foundation rank, often (though not always) consisting of stopped pipes. Also, (F.) **cor de nuit**.

nächtlich (G.) Dark, gloomy.

nach und nach (G.) Little by little, gradually, e.g., *nach und nach am Steg*, gradually play near (nearer) the bridge.

näherkommend (G.) Approaching, coming closer.

naïf, naïve (F.) Simple, artless. Also, **naïvement**.

narquois (F.) Cunning, sly.

narrante (It.) Recounting, telling.

narrativo (It.) Narrative.

nasard (F.) In organs, a rank of pipes that sound one octave and a fifth higher than the keys played. Also, **nazard, Nasat, octave quint, open twelfth, twelfth**.

Nase, aus der (G.) A nasal tone. Also, **durch die Nase, näselnd.**

natürlich (G.) Natural, simple, artless.

nazard (F.) Same as NASARD.

neckisch (G.) Playful, arch.

negra (Sp.) Quarter note.

nel, nell', nella, nello (It.) In the, inside, within, at, on, to.

ne—pas (F.) Do not, e.g., *ne hâtez pas*, do not hurry (not too fast).

nera (It.) Quarter note.

nerveux (F.) Excited, impatient, agitated. Also, **nerveusement.**

nervioso (Sp.) Agitated, vigorous, energetic.

nervös (G.) Agitated, excited, fidgety.

nervoso (It.) Restless, agitated. Also, **nervosamente.**

net (F.) Clearly, plainly, distinctly. Also, **nettement.**

netto (It.) Same as NET. Also, **nettamente.**

neu (G.) New, anew, again.

niaisement (F.) Foolishly.

nicht (G.) Not, e.g., *nicht zu langsam*, not too slow.

niente (It.) Nothing, e.g., *estinguendosi al niente*, dying away to nothing (no sound).

no (Sp.) Not, e.g., *no mucho*, not too much.

nobilmente (It.) Dignified, stately. Also, **nobile, con nobiltà.**

nobleza, con (Sp.) Nobly, with dignity.

noch (G.) Still, yet, e.g., *noch lauter*, still louder.

noch einmal (G.) Once more, again.

noire (F.) Quarter note.

non (F., It.) No, not.

nonchalamment (F.) Carelessly, easily. Also, **avec nonchalance.**

normale (It.) Indication to return to normal tuning, pitch, or octave, after scordatura, harmonics, etc. Also, **suono normale.**

nostalgico (It.) Longingly.

nostalgique (F.) Nostalgic, sentimental.

note blanche (F.) (1) Half note. (2) Occasionally, white key (on a keyboard instrument).

note noir (1) Quarter note. (2) Occasionally, black key (on a keyboard instrument).

nourri, bien (F.) With a rich, full tone.

nouveau, de (F.) Again.

nuance (F.) Shading, variety of intonation.

nuance, sans (F.) Very uniform, without shading.

nuovo, di (It.) Again.

O

o (1) (It., Sp.) Or. (2) (Port.) The.

obbligato (It.) In baroque music, an essential part. In some 19th-century music, an optional part.

oben (G.) Above, e.g., *wie (als) oben*, as above, as before.

obere (G.) (1) Upper (voice-part, manual, etc.). (2) Above.

Oboe (G.) Oboe.

oboe d'amore (It.) (1) Obsolete wind instrument. (2) In organs, a soft 8-foot manual reed stop. Also, **hautbois d'amour.**

occore (It.) As needed.

octavin (F.) (1) Piccolo. (2) An organ stop. Also, **piccolo.**

od (It.) Or.

oder (G.) Or.

Offenflöte (G.) In organs, a general name for an open flute stop.

ogni (It.) Every, e.g., *pedale ad ogni accordo,* pedal on every chord.

ohne (G.) Without, e.g., *ohne Pedal,* without pedal.

oíble (Sp.) Audible.

oiseau, comme un (F.) Like a bird.

Oktavflöte (G.) Piccolo.

ombre, dans l' (F.) In the background. Also, **à l'ombre.**

ondeggiando (It.) (1) Gently rocking. (2) In violin music, a wavery tremolo, or vibrato [see VIBRATO (1)].

ondoyant (F.) Flowing, undulating.

ondulado (Sp.) Rippling.

ondulando (It.) Rippling. Also, **ondulato.**

ongarese, all' (It.) In Hungarian (gypsy) style.

op. (L.) Short for OPUS.

opaco (It.) Dull, heavy.

opp. (It.) Short for OPPURE.

opprimente (It.) Oppressive, burdensome, crushing.

oppure (It.) Or else, indicating an alternative (usually easier) version. Also, **opp.**

opus (L.) Work. Also, **op.**

orageux (F.) Tempestuous.

oramai (It.) From now on, henceforth.

ordinario (It.) As usual, customary. Also, **d'ordinario, in modo ordinario.**

órgano (Sp.) Organ.

órgano de campanas (Sp.) Glockenspiel.

organo pleno (L.) Full organ.

Orgel (G.) Organ.

orgoglioso (It.) Haughty, proud, boastful.

orgue (F.) Organ.

orgueil, sans (F.) Without pride.

orlo, all' (It.) At the rim (of a drum, etc.).

orribile (It.) Loathsome, terrifying.

oscuro (It.) Dark, unclear.

ossessivo (It.) Obsessed.

ossia (It.) Or, or else, indicating an alternative version.

ostinato (It.) A steady bass accompaniment, repeated over and over. Also, **basso ostinato.**

ôter (F.) Remove, stop using (organ stops, mutes, etc.). Also, **ôtez.**

ottava (It.) Octave, usually meaning an octave higher or lower in pitch. Also, **8va, 8a, 8.**

ottava alta (It.) One octave higher.

ottava bassa (It.) One octave lower.

ottavino (It.) (1) Piccolo. (2) Soprano clarinet. (3) A small virginal (type of harpsichord).

ottetto (It.) Octet.

ottoni (It.) Brass section.

ou (F.) Or.

ouvert (F.) Open. Also, full-toned.

ouvert à moitié (F.) Half-open.

ovvero (It.) Or else, indicating an alternative version.

P

p (It.) Short for PIANO.

pabellon (Sp.) Bell (of horns, etc.), e.g., *pabellon en alto,* bells raised up.

pacato (It.) Calm, tranquil.

paisible (F.) Quiet, calm. Also, **paisiblement.**

palma, con la (Sp.) With the palm (of the hand).

palpitant (F.) Panting, quivering, fluttering.

palpitante (It.) Pulsating.

pandereta (Sp.) Tambourine.

panno (It.) A piece of cloth used to muffle a drum.

parejo (Sp.) Even, smooth.

parlando (It.) (1) In vocal music, a style approximating speech, usually in rapid tempo. (2) In instrumental music, in an expressive, declamatory style.

parlato (It.) (1) Spoken. (2) Same as parlando [see PARLANDO (1)].

parlé (F.) Spoken, speechlike.

parodia, con (It.) Parodying.

Parodie, mit (G.) Parodying, burlesquing.

parte (It.) (1) Voice-part, part. (2) Section.

parte, colla (It.) Follow the soloist's part, especially with regard to tempo.

partition (F.) Score.

Partitur (G.) Score.

pas, au (F.) At a walking pace, moderately slow.

pasión, con (Sp.) With great feeling. Also, **pasionero.**

passionato (It.) Impassioned, very expressive. Also, **con passione.**

passionné (F.) Fervent, passionate, heartfelt. Also, **avec passion, passionnément.**

pastorale (It.) In pastoral style.

pastoso (It.) Flowing, euphonious, with a mellow tone.

patètico (It.) With great emotion.

pathétique (F.) Same as PATÈTICO.

pathetisch (G.) Same as PATÈTICO. Also, **mit Pathos.**

Pathos, ohne (G.) Without feeling, unsentimental.

Pauken (G.) Timpani.

paume (F.) Palm (of the hand).

pauroso (It.) Timid, fearful.

pausa (It., Sp.) Rest, e.g., (It.) *pausa di bianca,* half rest.

pause (F.) Rest.

Pause (G.) Rest, e.g., *halbe Pause,* half rest, *viertel Pause,* quarter rest.

pavillon (F.) Bell (of wind instruments), e.g., *pavillons en (à) l'air,* with the bells raised.

peccaminoso (It.) Sinful.

ped. (It.) Short for PEDALE (1), (3).

Pedal (G.) Pedal.

pedale (It., Sp.) (1) Pedal (of organ, piano, harp, etc.). Also, **ped.** (2) Pedal point. (3) In organ music, indication to use pedals only. Also, **ped.**

pédale (F.) Pedal (of organ, piano, etc.).

pedale celeste (It.) Damper pedal.

pedale del forte (It.) Sustaining pedal.

pedale doppio (It.) Double (the part) on the pedal.

Pedalgebrauch, mit (G.) Using the pedal, with pedal.

Pedalwechsel (G.) Raise and depress pedal.

peine, à (F.) Hardly, scarcely.

penaud (F.) Sheepish, bashful, embarrassed.

pénétrant (F.) Keen, acute, sharp.

penetrante (It.) Acute, piercing.

penosamente (It.) Painfully, with difficulty, haltingly.

pensieroso (It.) Thoughtful, serious, solemn. Also, **pensoso.**

pensif, pensive (F.) Thoughtful.

pequeño, pequeña (Sp.) Little, small, brief, e.g., *pausa pequeña,* short rest.

perçant (F.) Piercing, penetrating.

percosso (It.) Struck, clashed.

percussione (It.) Percussion section.

percussivo (It.) Percussive, heavy.

percutant (F.) Explosive, percussive, forceful. Also, **percuté.**

percutido (Sp.) Struck, hammered, percussive.

perd. (It.) Short for PERDENDO.

perdant, en se (F.) Same as PERDENDO.

perdendo (It.) Dying away. Also, **perd., perdendosi.**

perdiéndose (Sp.) Same as PERDENDO. Also, **perdiéndosi.**

perdutamente (It.) Desperately, wildly.

perfido (It.) Also, **con perfidia.** (1) Treacherously. (2) Persistent repetition of a figure.

però (It.) Nevertheless, however, still, yet.

perpetuo (It.) Constant, perpetual, e.g., *moto perpetuo,* perpetual motion.

persiflierend (G.) Bantering, jesting, jocose.

pesado (Sp.) Heavy, slow, deliberate.

pesamment (F.) Same as PESADO.

pesant (F.) Same as PESADO.

pesante (It.) Weighty, ponderous, dull. Also, **pesantemente, con pesantezza.**

pesato (It.) Weighed, pondered. Also, **pesatamente.**

petite nasard (F.) In organs, a soft diapason or principal stop on the manuals.

petite trompette (F.) In organs, a moderately loud reed stop. Also, **echo trumpet.**

pettegolo (It.) Gossiping, tattling.

petulante (It.) Brash, conceited.

petulanza, con (It.) With arrogance, impertinently, pertly.

peu (F.) Little, a little. Also, **un peu.**

peu à peu (F.) Little by little, gradually.

peu pres, à (F.) Nearly, almost.

pfeifend (G.) Whistling.

pfiffig (G.) Crafty, artful.

Phantasieenmässig (G.) Like a fantasy.

phantastisch (G.) Fanciful.

phlegmatisch (G.) Slow-moving, phlegmatic.

phrasé (F.) Phrased.

phrasiert (G.) Phrased.

piacere, a (It.) Freely, at will, at the performer's discretion, especially with regard to tempo.

piacevole (It.) Pleasing, agreeable, graceful.

pianamente (It.) Smoothly, evenly.

piangendo (It.) Weeping.

pianissimo (It.) Very soft. Also, **pp, ppp.**

piano (It.) Soft. Also, **p.**

piatti (It.) Cymbals. Also, **piattiturchi.**

piccante (It.) Sharp, pointed.

picchiettato (It.) Same as PIQUÉ.

piccolo (It.) (1) Small. (2) In organs, an important flute stop. Also, **orchestral piccolo.**

pieghevole (It.) Flexible, accommodating.

piena (It.) Full, e.g., *piena voce,* full voice.

pièno (It.) (1) Full, same as PIENA. (2) Referring to diapason stops (of organs).

pietoso (It.) (1) Pitiful, wretched. (2) Loving, devoted.

pigrizia, con (It.) Lazily, idly.

pincé (F.) (1) Stiff, prim, mannered. (2) Plucked, same as PIZZICATO.

piqué (F.) (1) A short, quickly released note, similar to STACCATO. (2) In bowing, short detached notes produced without changing the direction of the bow.

più (It.) More, e.g., *più andante,* slower, *più forte,* louder.

più tosto (It.) Also, **piuttosto.** (1) More quickly. (2) Rather, somewhat.

pizzicato (It.) Plucked. Also, **pizz.**

placabile (It.) Soothing, mild.

placare (It.) To grow calm.

placido (It.) Calm, tranquil.

plaintif (F.) Mournful, plaintive. Also, **plaintivement.**

planer le chant, laissez (F.) Let the melody stand out.

plaqué (F.) Indication for notes of a chord to be played simultaneously (rather than in succession, as an arpeggio).

plat paume, à (F.) With the flat palm (of the hand).

plein, pleine (F.) Full, loud.

pleine sonorité, en (F.) With a full sound.

plein jeu (F.) In organs, an important mixture stop made up of open principal pipes.

pleno (It.) See PIÈNO.

pleurant, en (F.) Weeping, lamenting.

plötzlich (G.) Suddenly.

plus (F.) (1) More. (2) Also.

plus, le (F.) The most, e.g., *le plus vite possible,* as fast as possible.

plus encore (F.) Still more, e.g., *plus encore vif,* still livelier.

plus en plus, de (F.) More and more.

plus haut, comme (F.) As above, as before.

plûtot (F.) Rather, quite.

poco (It., Sp.) Little, a bit.

poco a poco (It., Sp.) Little by little, gradually.

poco meno (It.) A little less.

poderoso (Sp.) Powerful, loud.

poesia (It.) Lyrical.

poetico (It.) Poetic, lyrical.

poggiato (It.) Supported, leaning against.

poi (It.) Then, thenceforth, afterward.

poignant (F.) Heartfelt.

pointe, à la (F.) With the point of the bow.

pointu (F.) Sharp, shrill.

polacca, alla (It.) In Polish style (of a mazurka, etc.).

pollice, col (It.) With the thumb.

Pommer (G.) In organs, same as GEDECKTPOMMER.

pompa, con (It.) With pomp, ostentatiously.

pompeux, pompeuse (F.) Stately, solemn.

pomphaft (G.) Grandiose, showy, pompous.

pompös (G.) Magnificent, splendid.

pomposo (It.) Stately, majestic.

ponctué (F.) Punctuated, accented, marked.

ponticello, sul (It.) Over the bridge (of violins, etc.), producing a nasal, brittle tone.

popular (Sp.) Popular, folklike, e.g., *con sentimiento popular,* in the style of folk music.

portamento (It.) A glide from one note to another.

portando la voce (It.) Carrying the voice over.

portato (It.) Half-staccato.

portez (F.) Hold, carry over, tie.

portez la voix (F.) In singing, gliding from one note to the next, in a continuous sound. Also, **port de voix.**

Portunalflöte (G.) In organs, same as BORDUNALFLÖTE.

Posaune (G.) (1) Trombone. (2) In organs, an important chorus reed stop whose tone is much like the orchestral trombone's.

posément (F.) Sedate, stately.

positif (F.) Positive organ (or choir organ).

possibile (It.) Possible, e.g., *il più presto possibile,* as fast as possible.

possierlich (G.) Droll, clowning, comical.

pouce, avec le (F.) With the thumb.

poussez (F.) Up-bow.

pp (It.) Short for PIANISSIMO. Also, **ppp.**

prachtvoll (G.) Splendid, magnificent.

précaution, avec (F.) Warily, cautiously.

précédent (F.) Former, foregoing, preceding.

precipitado (Sp.) Hasty, abrupt.

precipitando (It.) Rushing ahead, impetuous.

precipitar (Sp.) Same as PRECIPITANDO.

precipité (F.) Same as PRECIPITANDO.

precipitoso (It.) Same as PRECIPITANDO.

précis (F.) Exact, precise, rather terse.

preciso (It.) Exact, very accurate, precise. Also, **con precisione.**

preghevole (It.) Pleadingly.

premier, première (F.) First. Also, Ier, Iere.

près de (F.) Near, nearby, e.g., *près du chevalet,* near the bridge.

presque (F.) Almost, e.g., *presque parlé,* almost spoken, *presque rien,* hardly at all, scarcely.

pressa, sem (Sp.) Without haste.

pressando (It.) Pressing on, hurrying, accelerating. Also, **pressante, pressare.**

pressant, en (F.) Hurrying, quite fast. Also, **pressez, presser.**

prestant (F.) Diapason.

preste (F.) Very fast and agile. Also, **prestement.**

prestissimo (It.) As fast as possible.

presto (It.) Fast, faster than allegro, the fastest of the conventional tempos.

prima, primo (It., Sp.) First, principal, original, e.g., *tempo primo,* original tempo, (It.) *flauto primo,* first flute. Also, **I°.**

primitivo (It.) (1) Original, e.g., *tempo primitivo,* original tempo. (2) Simple, plain, crude.

principale (It.) Chief part, solo.

principio (It.) Beginning, e.g., *dal principio al fine,* from beginning to end, *come in principio,* as at the beginning.

profondo (It.) (1) Profound, deep. (2) Low-pitched.

progressivement (F.) Progressively, increasingly.

prolungando (It.) Extending, sustaining.

prononciert (G.) Pronounced, enunciated.

pronto (It., Sp.) Promptly, swiftly.

pronunziato (It.) Enunciated.

proprement (F.) Neatly, suitably.

prorompendo (It.) Bursting out.

prunkvoll (G.) Pompously, ostentatiously.

psalmodie, comme une (F.) Like a psalm, intoned. Also, **en psalmodiant.**

puente (Sp.) Bridge (of violins, etc.).

puissant (F.) Forceful, loud.

pulgar (Sp.) Thumb.

pulsando (It.) Throbbing, beating, pulsating.

pungente (It.) Biting, sharp, poignant.

punta, a (It.) With the point of the bow. Also, **a punta d'arco.**

puntato (It.) (1) Dotted, staccato. (2) A simplifed arrangement.

pur (F.) Clear, straightforward.

Q

quadruple-croche (F.) Sixty-fourth note.

quanto (It.) Much, how much, as much.

quart de soupir (F.) Sixteenth rest.

quasi (It.) Almost, as if, e.g., *quasi campane,* almost like bells, *quasi niente,* almost nothing (i.e., very soft).

quatre (F.) Four, e.g., *à quatre mains,* for four hands (a keyboard duet).

quattro (It.) Four, e.g., *a quattro mani,* for four hands.

quatuor (F.) Quartet.

que (1) (F., Sp.) That, which, who, whom, etc. (2) (F.) Than, as if, whether, e.g., *moins que,* less than. (3) (Sp.) Let, allow, e.g., *que se oigu el canto,* let the melody be heard (stress the melody).

Querflöte (G.) (1) Older name for orchestral flute. (2) In organs, same as FLAUTO TRAVERSO.

questo (It.) This.

quieto (It.) Quiet, hushed.

quillio (It.) Falsetto.

quint (F.) In organs, a foundation stop that sounds a fifth higher than the keys played. Also, **fifth, gross nasard.**

quintade (F.) In organs, an important stopped metal flute stop.

quintaton (F.) An organ stop.

Quintaten (G.) In organs, a stopped flute stop that varies widely from organ to organ.

quintette (F.) Quintet. Also, **quintuor.**

quittez (F.) Stop, leave off. Also, **quitter.**

R

rabbia, con (It.) With fury, enraged, violent. Also, **rabbioso.**

raccontando (It.) Narrated.

raddolcendo (It.) Becoming softer.

raddoppiando (It.) Double, e.g., *radoppiando il canto,* double the vocal part (with instruments).

radieux (F.) Radiant, brilliant.

radouci (F.) Softer, gentler.

raffrenando (It.) Slowing down.

rageur, avec (F.) With furor, passionately. Also, **rageusement.**

raggiungere (It.) To reach, to attain, e.g., *raggiungere il tempo* ♩ = *150,* speed up until reaching the tempo of 150 quarter notes per minute.

ralentir (F.) To slow down. Also, **ralentissement.**

rallentando (It.) Becoming slower. Also, **rall.**

ramenez le mouvement (F.) Return to tempo.

ranimant (F.) Reviving, becoming livelier.

Rankett (G.) In organs, an important reed stop.

rapidamente (It.) Quickly. Also, **rapido.**

rapide (F.) Fast.

rápido (Sp.) Fast.

rappresentativo (It.) (1) Expressive, illustrative. (2) Typical, representative. (3) Referring to *stile rappresentativo,* a style of recitative used in early operas as well as other vocal music from about 1600 to 1650.

rapprochant, en se (F.) Approaching, coming together.

rapsodico (It.) Rhapsodically.

rasch (G.) Quick.

Raserei, mit (G.) With frenzy, enraged. Also, **rasend.**

rasgueado (Sp.) Embellished, ornamented; in guitar music, playing flourishes.

rasquedo (Sp.) Rasping, scraping.

rassegnato (It.) Resigned, reconciled, meek. Also, **con rassegnazione.**

rasserenandosi (It.) Brightening.

rattenendo (It.) Slowing down, holding back. Also, **rattenuto.**

rauco (It.) Hoarse, strident.

rauh (G.) Rough, harsh.

rauschend (G.) (1) Rustling, murmuring. (2) Roaring, swelling.

Rauschquinte (G.) In organs, a compound stop made up of diapason ranks.

ravissement, avec (F.) Rapturously.

ravivé (F.) Revived, livelier.

ravvivando (It.) Quickening, brightening.

rechte Hand (G.) Right hand. Also, **R.H.**

récit (F.) (1) Recitative. Also, **récitatif.** (2) An organ manual, in English called **swell organ.**

recit. (It.) Short for RECITATIVO.

recitando (It.) Singing.

récitant (F.) Soloist, solo.

recitativo (It.) Recitative.

recité (F.) Performed as a recitative; spoken.

recueilli (F.) Meditative, contemplative.

reculant (F.) Receding, delaying.

redoblante (Sp.) Tenor drum.

redonda (Sp.) Whole note.

réduction (F.) Short score.

regagnant le Ier mouvement, en (F.) Returning to the first tempo.

regelmässig (G.) Uniform, even.

religioso (It.) Sacred, devout.

renforcer (F.) To reinforce or augment, to grow louder. Also, **renforcez.**

répétez (F.) Repeat.

replica (It.) Repeat.

reprenez (F.) Resume, e.g., *reprenez le mouvement,* resume tempo.

reprise (F.) A repeat.

requebrando (Sp.) Flirtatious, ingratiating.

resbalad (Sp.) Sliding, a glissando.

résigné (F.) Resigned, submissive.

résolu (F.) Determined, bold.

résonné (F.) With full sound, resounding. Also, **résonner.**

respecter le doigté (F.) Follow the fingering.

respingendo (It.) Driving back, repelling.

respiro (It.) Breath.

ressortir (F.) To emphasize.

restez (F.) Remain, stay there, usually referring to a string or finger position.

resuelto (Sp.) Resolute, determined.

retardant, en (F.) Slowing down.

retardar (Sp.) To slow down.

retenant (F.) Holding back, slowing down. Also, **retenez, retenu.**

retenido (Sp.) Same as RETENANT. Also, **retener, reteniendo.**

retournez (F.) Return.

retranchez (F.) Cut short, suppress.

rêve (F.) Dream.

revenez (F.) Return, e.g., *revenez au mouvement,* return to tempo.

rêveur (F.) Dreamy, pensive. Also, **rêveuse, rêveusement.**

Rezitativ (G.) Recitative. Also, **Recitatif.**

rezitativartig (G.) In the manner of a recitative.

rezitieren (G.) To recite.

rf, rfz (It.) Short for RINFORZANDO.

R.H. (G.) Short for right hand.

rhytmisch (G.) Rhythmical, lilting.

rianimando (It.) Reviving, becoming lively.

ricochet (F.) Same as JETÉ.

ricordando (It.) Remembering.

rideau (F.) Curtain (of a stage).

ridendo (It.) Laughing.

rigido de movimento (It.) In strict time.

rigo (It.) Staff.

rigoglioso (It.) Exuberant, vigorous.

rigor de compasso (Port.) Strict time.

rigoroso (It.) Strictly, in strict time. Also, **con rigore, rigorosamente.**

rigoureux (F.) Strict, precise.

rigueur (F.) Strictness, e.g. *à la rigueur,* strictly (as written), *sans rigueur,* not strictly, freely.

rilasciando (It.) Slowing down.

rilassando (It.) Relaxing, slackening, slowing down.

rilievo, in (It.) Standing out, emphasized. Also, **rilevato.**

rimbrottando (It.) Taunting, reproaching.

rimettendosi (It.) Renewed, revived, resumed (an earlier tempo).

rinforzando (It.) A sudden accent, same as SFORZANDO. Also, **rinforzato, rinf., rf., rfz.**

ripetizione (It.) A repeat.

ripieni, senza (It.) The first player of each section only (first horn, first oboe, etc.).

ripieno (It.) (1) In organs, a mixture stop. (2) In a concerto grosso, the full orchestra.

ripigliando (It.) Reviving, resuming.

riposo, con (It.) Restful, peaceful.

riprendendo (It.) Resuming, returning to, e.g., *riprendendo il I° tempo,* return to the original tempo.

risoluto (It.) Boldly, decisively, vigorously.

risonante (It.) Resounding, ringing, sonorous.

risonare (It.) Also, **risuonare.** (1) To resound, to echo, to continue sounding. (2) To repeat (a note, passage, etc.).

risvegliato (It.) Revived, faster.

ritardando (It.) Becoming slower. Also, **ritard., rit.**

ritenuto (It.) Immediately slower, held back. Also, **riten.**

ritmico (It.) Rhythmic, in strict time.

rítmico (Sp.) Rhythmic.

ritmo (It., Sp.) Rhythm.

ritmo, a gran (Sp.) Very fast.

ritornando (It.) Returning. Also, **ritornate.**

ritraendosi (It.) Representing, depicting.

riverbero (It.) Echo, reverberation.

riverso (It.) (1) Inversion. (2) Retrograde motion.

robust (G.) Sturdy, strong, firm, bold.

robustement (F.) Vigorously.

robusto (It.) Same as ROBUST.

roco (It.) Hoarse.

roh (G.) Rough, crude.

Rohr (G.) In organs, referring to various pipes that are half-covered (or half-open), e.g., **Rohrgedeckt, Rohrschalmei,** etc.

Rohrbordun (G.) In organs, a half-covered flute stop.

Rohrflöte (G.) In organs, a half-covered solo and ensemble flute stop. Also, **chimney flute.**

Rohrpommer (G.) In organs, a half-covered GEDECKTPOMMER of large scale.

rollante (It.) Rolling (like a ship).

ronde (F.) Whole note.

rondement (F.) Quickly, briskly.

rubato (It.) Taking a portion of the time value from one note and giving it to another note (usually) within the same measure, without altering the duration of the measure as a whole. Also, **tempo rubato.**

Rückerinnerung (G.) Reminiscence.

rückkehrend (G.) Returning, reverting.

rücksichtslos (G.) Reckless, heedless, without consideration. Also, **ohne Rücksicht.**

rude (F., It.) Rough, harsh, unevenly. Also, (F.) **rudement,** (It.) **con rudezza.**

rufend (G.) Calling.

ruhelos (G.) Restless, disquieted.

ruhevoll (G.) Restful, calm.

ruhig (G.) Quiet, soft. Also, **mit Ruhe.**

Rührtrommel (G.) Tenor drum.

Rührung (G.) Deep feeling. Also, **rührend.**

rumor, como un (Sp.) Like a murmur, buzzing.

rumoroso (Sp.) Loud, rumbling.

russico, nel modo (It.) In Russian style.

rustico (It.) Rustic, plain, simple.

ruvido (It.) Rough, coarse. Also, **ruvidamente, con ruvidezza.**

rythmé (F.) Measured, in precise rhythm.

rythme brisé (F.) Broken rhythm, uneven.

S

saccadé (F.) Abrupt, jerky.

Saite (G.) String.

salicional (F.) An organ stop.

salmodiando (It.) Intoning, psalm-like.

saltando (It.) Same as SAUTILLÉ. Also, **saltato.**

saltellante (It.) Skipping, tripping lightly. Also, **saltellato.**

sanft (G.) Soft, gentle.

sans (F.) Without.

sardonico (It.) Sneering, sarcastic.

sassofone (It.) Saxophone.

satanico (It.) Devilish, satanic, evil.

satirico (It.) Mocking, satirical.

satt (G.) Full, satisfied, e.g., *mit sattem Ton*, with a full tone.

Satz (G.) Movement (of a sonata, symphony, etc.).

sauté de la pointe (F.) Bounced against the strings with the tip of the bow.

sautillant (F.) Jerky, skipping.

sautillé (F.) In bowing, a short rapid stroke that makes the bow bounce lightly off the string.

sauvage (F.) Wild, untamed.

saxófono (Sp.) Saxophone. Also, **saxofón.**

sbeffeggiando (It.) Mocking.

sbloccata (It.) Released.

scalpitante (It.) Pounding, galloping.

scampanatino (It.) Tinkling, bell-like.

scandé (F.) Scanned, broken up into separate units of rhythm and meter, syllabic.

scandendo (It.) Ascending.

scandito, ben (It.) Pronounced distinctly, well articulated. Also, **scandire.**

scatenato (It.) Unleashed, tempestuous.

scattando (It.) Bursting out.

schalkhaft (G.) Roguish, sly.

Schalltrichter (G.) Bells (of wind instruments).

Schalmei (G.) In organs, an important reed stop, resembling the tone of the medieval shawm. Also, **shawm,** (F.) **chalumeau.**

scharf (G.) (1) Sharp, sudden. (2) *cap*. In organs, same as ACUTA.

scharrend (G.) Scratching, scraping.

schattenhaft (G.) Subtly blended, shaded. Also, **schattig.**

schaudernd (G.) Shuddering, trembling.

schelmisch (G.) Sly, roguish, arch.

scherzando (It.) Playfully, jestingly. Also, **scherzevole, scherzoso.**

scherzhaft (G.) Playful, jocular. Also, **scherzend.**

scherzo (It.) Referring to the tempo and mood of a scherzo movement, i.e., lively and brisk.

schiamazzando (It.) Squawking, clamoring, in a continual uproar.

schianto, come uno (It.) Like a crash or a sudden blow.

schiettamente (It.) Openly, simply, plainly.

Schlag (G.) A stroke, a blow.

schlagen (G.) To strike.

Schlagwerk (G.) Percussion section. Also, **Schlaginstrumente.**

schleichend (G.) Creeping, furtive.

schleppend (G.) Dragging, slow.

schlicht (G.) Plain, straightforward, smooth, e.g., *mit schlichtem Vortrag,* perform smoothly.

schluchzend (G.) Sobbing.

Schluss (G.) End, e.g., *bis zum Schluss,* up to the end.

schmachtend (G.) Languishing, yearning.

schmeichelnd (G.) Coaxing, flattering.

schmelzend (G.) (1) Sweet, melodious. (2) Diminishing.

schmerzlich (G.) Painful, distressed.

schmetternd (G.) (1) Loud, blaring. (2) In horn playing, a harsh, brassy tone.

Schnarrsaite (G.) Snarehead (of a snare drum).

schneidend (G.) Cutting, sharp, biting.

schnell (G.) Fast. Also, **Schnelligkeit,** speed.

schneller (G.) (1) Faster. (2) *cap.* Inverted mordent.

schnippish (G.) Pert, snappish.

Schöngedeckt (G.) In organs, a stopped flute stop.

schreitend (G.) Striding, moving slowly and steadily.

schrittmässig (G.) Measured, even.

schroff (G.) Gruff, harsh.

schwach (G.) Weak, soft.

Schwammschlager (G.) Sponge-headed drumstick.

schwärmerisch (G.) With enthusiasm, wild.

schwebend (G.) Light, lilting, uneven.

schwelgend (G.) Voluptuous.

schwer (G.) Heavy, serious, ponderous.

schweren Akzenten, mit (G.) With heavy accents.

schwerfällig (G.) Heavy, slow.

schwermütig (G.) Melancholy, moody.

schwindend (G.) Dying away.

Schwung, mit (G.) Lively, with verve. Also, **schwungvoll.**

scintillant (F.) Sparkling, brilliant. Also, (F., It.) **scintillante.**

sciolto (It.) Easy, unconstrained, fluent. Also, **scioltamente.**

scolpito (It.) Clear and distinct. Also, **scolpitante.**

scomparendo (It.) Disappearing, vanishing.

scoperto (It.) Exposed, bare, clear.

scordato (It.) Out of tune, off pitch.

scordatura (It.) Deliberate change in tuning.

scorrendo (It.) Flowing, gliding. Also, **scorrevole.**

scucito (It.) Unconnected, detached, opposite of LEGATO.

scuro (It.) Dark, gloomy.

sdegnoso (It.) Haughty, scornful.

sdrucciolando (It.) Slippery, sliding.

sea pueda (Sp.) As possible.

sec, sèche (F.) Curt, dry, abrupt. Also, **avec sécheresse.**

secco (It.) Plain, simple, unadorned.

Sechzehntel (G.) Sixteenth note.

seco (Sp.) Dry, concise.

secondaire (F.) Secondary.

seelenvoll (G.) Soulful, heartfelt.

segno (It.) Sign, meaning the sign 𝄋. Thus, *al segno,* to the sign, *dal segno,* from the sign.

segreto (It.) Hidden, furtive.

segue (It.) Continue without pausing.

seguendo l'azione (It.) Following the action (on stage).

seguidilla (Sp.) A traditional Spanish dance.

seguire il canto (It.) Follow the melody (vocal part, solo).

sehnsuchtsvoll (G.) With longing, wistful. Also, **sehnsüchtig, mit Sehnsucht.**

sehr (G.) Very, e.g., *sehr langsam,* very slow.

seizième de soupir (F.) Sixty-fourth rest.

selbe (G.) Same, e.g., *das selbe Zeitmass,* the same tempo.

selig (G.) Blissful, happy, heavenly.

selon (F.) According to.

selvaggio (It.) Wild, savage, boisterous. Also, **selvaggiamente.**

sem (Port.) Without.

semibiscroma (It.) Sixty-fourth note.

semibreve (It.) Whole note.

semicorchea (Sp.) Sixteenth note.

semicroma (It.) Sixteenth note.

semifusa (Sp.) Sixty-fourth note.

semp. (It.) Short for SEMPRE.

semplice (It.) Simple, unaffected. Also, **con semplicità.**

sempre (It., Port.) Always, continually, throughout, e.g., (It.) *sempre dopo la voce,* always following the voice (vocal part).

sencillamente (Sp.) Simply, plainly. Also, **con sencillez.**

sensibile (It.) (1) Sensitive, tender. (2) The leading tone. Also, **nota sensibile.**

sentido (Sp.) Heard, audible.

sentiment (F.) Feeling, mood, e.g., *avec un sentiment émouvant,* with deep feeling.

sentimento, con (It.) With feeling. Also, **sentimentale.**

sentimiento (Sp.) (1) With feeling. (2) Sorrowful.

sentito (It.) (1) Heard. (2) Expressive, heartfelt, warm.

senza (It.) Without.

separado (Sp.) Same as DETACHÉ.

separato (It.) Detached.

separez (F.) Separate, uncouple (in organs).

septadecima (L.) In organs, same as TIERCE.

septième (F.) In organs, a foundation rank of soft open metal pipes, which sound two octaves and a minor seventh higher than the keys played. Also, **twenty-first, flatted.**

septuor (F.) Septet.

Seraphonflöte (G.) In organs, an open flute stop. Also, **Jubalflöte.**

serein (F.) Placid, tranquil.

serenidad (Sp.) Calm, peaceful.

sereno (It.) Same as SERENIDAD. Also, **serenamente, con serenità.**

serietà, con (It.) Seriously, earnestly, gravely. Also, **serioso.**

serrer (F.) To condense, to speed up. Also, **serrez, serre, en serrant.**

sesquialtera (It.) In organs, an important mixture stop, usually made up of diapason pipes.

sestetto (It.) Sextet.

settimino (It.) Septet.

Seufzer, wie ein (G.) Like a sigh.

seul, seule (F.) Alone.

seulement (F.) Only.

severo (It.) Strict, rigid.

sf, sfz (It.) Short for SFORZANDO.

sfp (It.) Short for SFORZANDO-PIANO, accented, then soft.

sferzante (It.) Rebuking, punishing.

sfida (It.) Defiance, e.g., *con accento di sfida,* with a defiant air.

sfiorato (It.) Touching lightly, skimming over, caressing.

sfogato (It.) (1) Let loose, freed. (2) Exhaled; in singing, very light and airy.

sfoggiando (It.) Ostentatious, lavish.

sfolgorante (It.) Flashing, brilliant.

sforzando (It.) With a strong accent. Also, **rinforzando, sforzato, sf., sfz.**

sforzata (It.) Forced, e.g., *sforzata gaiezza,* forced gaiety.

sforzato (It.) Same as SFORZANDO.

sfrenato (It.) Unrestrained, wild.

sfumando (It.) Fading away, gradually diminishing.

sgarbatamente (It.) Rudely, awkwardly.

sguaiato (It.) Rude, coarse. Also, **sguaiatamente.**

sibillino (It.) Mysterious, cryptic.

siciliano (It.) A Sicilian dance in 6/8 meter and fairly slow tempo.

sicurezza, con (It.) With assurance. Also, **sicuro.**

sieghaft (G.) Victorious.

siempre (Sp.) Always, constantly.

sifflant (F.) (1) Hissing, whistling. (2) Flutter tonguing.

Sifflöte (G.) In organs, a manual flute stop with a brilliant tone.

signe (F.) Sign, usually 𝄋

sigue (Sp.) Continue without pause.

silbern (G.) Silvery, with a clear, bell-like tone.

silencio (Sp.) Rest, e.g., *silencio de negra,* quarter rest.

silenzio (It.) Silence, a rest.

sillabando (It.) Pronouncing by syllables.

sillabato, ben (It.) Clearly articulated.

simile (It.) Similarly, in like manner. Also, **sim.**

simple (F.) Plain, simple, artless. Also, **simplement.**

sin (Sp.) Without.

sin' (It.) Up to, until.

sine (L.) Without.

singend (G.) Singing, melodious, CANTABILE. Also, **singbar.**

singhiozzando (It.) Sobbing, hiccupping.

singhiozzo, come un (It.) (1) Like a sob or hiccup. (2) The device of hocket.

sinistra (It.) Left (hand). Also, **mano sinistra, m.s.**

sino (It.) Up to, until.

sinuoso (It.) Smooth, curving.
sipario (It.) Curtain (of a stage).
slancio, con (It.) Vigorously, with dash.
slargando (It.) Slowing down.
slentando (It.) Slackening, slowing down.
slontando (It.) Withdrawing, becoming softer.
smanioso (It.) Frenzied.
smarrito (It.) Bewildered, confused.
sminuendo (It.) Becoming softer.
smorendo (It.) Dying away.
smorfioso (It.) Affected, mincing.
smorzando (It.) Fading away. Also, **smorz.**
snèllo (It.) Nimble, agile, brisk.
so (G.) As, e.g., *doppelt so schnell*, twice as fast.
soave (It.) Gentle, sweet, delicate. Also, **soavemente.**
soavissimo (It.) As sweetly (gently, delicately) as possible.
sobre (Sp.) On, over, above, e.g., *sobre el puente*, over the bridge.
sobresaliendo (Sp.) Emphasizing, standing out.
sobrio (Sp.) Sober, restrained.
sofferente (It.) (1) Suffering, ill. (2) Patient, enduring.
soffice (It.) Light, gentle, soft.
soffio, come un (It.) Like a breath, very light.
soffocato (It.) Smothered, stifled, damped. Also, **con voce soffocata.**
sofort (G.) Immediately, at once, e.g., *sofort anschliessen*, connect immediately (continue without pause).

sognando (It.) Dreaming, musing. Also, **sognante.**
sogno, come un (It.) Like a dream, illusive.
soigneusement (F.) Carefully, elegantly. Also, **soigneuxment, avec soin.**
soignez le son (F.) Refine the tone.
solaire (F.) Sunny, bright.
solenne (It.) Very serious, stately. Also, **con solennità.**
solennel (F.) Solemn, sedate.
solo (It., L., Sp.) (1) Single, alone, a part performed by one performer. (2) In organs, term for various stops of more conspicuous tone color than the average rank of the same name, e.g., **solo tibia clausa, solo tuba,** etc.
sombre (F.) Melancholy, gloomy.
sombrío (Sp.) Gloomy, somber.
somma (It.) Highest, utmost.
sommesso (It.) Subdued, soft.
somnolent (F.) Drowsy, relaxed.
son (F.) Tone, sound, e.g., *à plein son*, with a full tone.
sonabile (It.) (1) Playable. (2) Sonorous, ringing, resonant.
son harmonique (F.) Harmonic (overtone).
sonido (Sp.) Sound, tone.
sonido natural (Sp.) Natural tone; in violins, etc., open tone.
sonnacchioso (It.) Sleepy, sluggish.
sonore (F.) Resonant.
sonorité (F.) Resonance, tone quality.
sonoro (It.) Resonant, full-toned. Also, **sonoramente.**

sopra (It.) Over, above, e.g., *come sopra,* as above (as before).

sordamente (It.) Muted, very soft. Also, **sordo.**

sordina (Sp.) Mute or damper.

sordino (It.) Mute or damper, e.g., *con sordini,* with mutes or damper (pedal), *senza sordini,* without mutes or damper.

sordo (Sp.) Muffled.

sorgendo (It.) Rising, emerging, becoming louder.

sorglos (G.) Carefree.

sospeso (It.) Suspended.

sospettoso (It.) Suspicious, wary, dubious.

sospirando (It.) Sighing, plaintive. Also, **sospirato.**

sostenido (Sp.) Same as SOSTENUTO.

sostenuto (It.) Sustained. Also, **sost.**

sotto (It.) Under, below.

sotto voce (It.) Softly, in a low voice.

soubasse (F.) In organs, the principal stopped bass stop, with a big, intense tone. Also, **contra bourdon, sub bass, sub bourdon,** (G.) **Untersatz.**

soudainement (F.) Suddenly. Also, **soudain.**

souffle (F.) Breath, e.g., *dans un souffle,* in one breath, *comme un souffle,* like a breath, very light.

souffrant (F.) Suffering, grieving. Also, **avec souffrance.**

soupir (F.) (1) Quarter rest. (2) Sigh, breath, gasp.

soupirant (F.) Sighing, plaintive.

souple (F.) Flexible, smooth. Also, **souplement, avec souplesse.**

sourd (F.) Dull, muffled, muted. Also, **sourdement.**

sourdine (F.) Mute or damper.

soutenu (F.) Sustained, held.

sparire (It.) To fade away.

spavalderia, con (It.) Impudently, defiantly. Also, **spavaldo.**

spaziato (It.) Ranging freely, wandering.

spazzole (It.) Brushes (used with percussion instruments). Also, **con spazzola.**

spegnendosi (It.) Dying away.

spegnere il suono (It.) To stop the sound, to become silent.

spensieratamente (It.) Thoughtlessly, freely.

speranza, senza (It.) Without hope, lacking confidence.

sperdendosi (It.) Fading away.

spianato (It.) Smooth, even, sustained.

spiccato (It.) In bowing, a light staccato played between the frog and the midpoint of the bow, at slow to moderate speed.

spiegato (It.) With full voice and becoming louder. Also, **a voce spiegata.**

spielerisch (G.) Playful, jocular.

spietato (It.) Ruthless, cruel.

spigliato (It.) Free and easy, graceful.

Spillflöte (G.) In organs, an open flute stop. Also, **Spindelflöte.**

Spindelflöte (G.) Same as SPILLFLÖTE.

spingendo (It.) (1) Driving ahead. (2) Up-bowing.

spirando (It.) Breathing, exhaling.

Spireflöte (G.) In organs, same as SPITZFLÖTE.

spiritoso (It.) Spirited, lively. Also, **con spirito.**

spiritu, con (L.) Wth spirit.

spitz (G.) (1) Sharp, biting. Also, **spitzig.** (2) *cap.* Point of the bow. Also, **Spitze.**

Spitzflöte (G.) In organs, an important open flute stop. Also, **Spireflöte.**

Spitzprinzipal (G.) In organs, an important foundation stop, made up of slightly conical pipes. Also, **cone diapason, Spitz diapason.**

spottisch (G.) Mocking, sarcastic.

sprezzante (It.) Haughty, disdainful. Also, **con sprezzo.**

springend (G.) Bouncing. In bowing, *mit springendem Bogen,* bouncing the bow against the strings, as in SAUTILLÉ.

spugna (It.) Sponge, e.g., *bacchette di spugna,* spongeheaded drumsticks.

squarciagola, a (It.) At the top of the voice, yelling.

squillante (It.) Ringing, pealing.

staccato (It.) Detached, with each note separated from the next and quickly released. Also, **stacc.**

stammelnd (G.) Stammering, faltering.

stampfend (G.) Stamping, pounding.

stancamente (It.) Wearily, slowly. Also, **stanco, con stanchezza.**

stark (G.) (1) Strong, vigorous, loud. (2) Very, e.g, *stark bewegt,* very lively.

starr (G.) Rigid, inflexible.

statico (It.) Steady, unchanging.

Steg, am (G.) On (near) the bridge.

steigernd (G.) Augmenting, becoming louder. Also, **in Steigerung.**

Stelle (G.) Place, e.g., *an der selben Stelle,* in the same place.

stendendo (It.) Slowing down.

stentando (It.) Difficult, labored, slow. Also, **stentato, stent.**

Stenthorn (G.) In organs, a loud 8-foot manual solo stop.

Stentor (G.) In organs, name for various stops that are unusually loud and powerful, e.g., **Stentorflöte, Stentor gamba,** etc.

sterbend (G.) Dying away.

steso (It.) Slow, broad.

stesso (It.) Same.

stetig (G.) Same as STETS.

stets (G.) Continually, always, e.g., *stets arpeggieren,* continually (play) broken chords. Also, **stetig.**

still (G.) Quiet, soft.

Stimme (G.) (1) Voice, e.g., *mit erregter Stimme,* in an agitated voice. (2) Voice-part.

Stimmung (G.) (1) Mood. (2) Tuning.

stinguendo (It.) Fading away.

stiracchiando (It.) Drawing out, slowing down. Also, **stirato.**

stirato (It.) Same as STIRACCHIANDO.

stizzoso (It.) Petulant, spiteful.

stockend (G.) Hesitating, haltingly, slackening in tempo.

stolz (G.) Stately, majestic.

straff (G.) Rigid, tense, concise.

strahlend (G.) Beaming, radiant.

strappata (It.) Plucked, strummed. Also, **strappate, strappato.**

strasciando (It.) Dragging. Also, **strascicamente.**

strascinando (It.) Also, **strascinare, strascinato.** (1) Drawling, drawing out, dragging. (2) A glissando or portamento, i.e., sliding from one note to another.

stravaganza, con (It.) Whimsically, fancifully. Also, **stravagante.**

straziante (It.) Anguished, tortured. Also, **straziando, con strazio.**

streichen (G.) To bow, e.g., *breit streichen,* bow broadly (with long broad strokes).

Streicher (G.) String section. Also, **Streichinstrumente.**

streng (G.) Strict, exact, e.g., *streng im Takt,* in strict tempo.

strepitoso (It.) Noisy, boisterous. Also, **con strepito.**

stretta (It.) A STRETTO passage.

stretta, alla (It.) Faster.

stretto (It.) (1) Accelerated, faster. (2) A concluding section in faster tempo. (3) In contrapuntal music, the device of speeding up imitation by the various parts.

Strich (G.) Stroke, bow stroke.

strictement (F.) Strictly, exactly, e.g., *strictement en mesure,* in strict time.

stridente (It.) Shrill, shrieking. Also, **stridulo.**

stringendo (It.) Pressing on, hurrying, speeding up. Also, **stringente, string.**

strisciando (It.) A glide from one note to the next.

strisciata (It.) Rubbing, stroking, sliding (for cymbals, etc.).

strömend (G.) Flowing.

strozzata (It.) Strangled, choking.

stumm (G.) Mute, silent.

stürmisch (G.) Stormy, violent, passionate.

Stürze (G.) Bell (of wind instrument).

su, arco in (It.) Up-bow.

suadente (It.) Persuasive, convincing.

suave (Sp.) Smooth, gentle, soft.

subit, subite (F.) Sudden, suddenly.

subito (It.) Suddenly, immediately, at once.

súbito (Sp.) Sudden.

subtil (1) (F.) Subtle, acute. (2) (G.) Subtle, delicate.

suelto (Sp.) Loose, free, flowing.

suivant (F.) According to, following.

suivez (F.) (1) Continue next section without pause. (2) Follow the soloist, especially with regard to tempo.

sul, sulla, sulle (It.) On the.

suonare (It.) To sound, e.g., *lasciar suonare,* let (continue) to sound.

suonare a fantasia (It.) Improvise.

suono (It.) Musical sound, e.g., *senza suono,* without music (i.e., spoken).

suppliant (F.) Beseeching, entreating.

sur (F.) On, over, e.g., *sur la touche*, over the fingerboard.

suspirante (Sp.) Sighing, longingly.

süss (G.) Sweet, melodious.

sussurro (It.) Whisper, murmur. Also, **sussurrando, sussurrato.**

susteniendo (Sp.) Sustaining, holding, e.g., *susteniendo con los pedales,* sustain with the pedals.

svagato (It.) Absentminded, heedless.

svanendo (It.) Fading away.

svegliando (It.) Awakening, becoming agitated.

svelto (It.) Brisk, light, lively.

T

table (F.) Soundboard, belly.

tace (It.) Be silent.

tacet (L.) Be silent.

tagliente (It.) Sharp, keen.

Takt (G.) (1) Measure, bar, e.g., *Pedal jeden Takt,* use pedal for each measure. (2) Beat, meter, time, e.g., 3/4 *Takt,* 3/4 meter. (3) Tempo.

Takt, im (G.) In strict time.

Takt, ohne (G.) In free rhythm and time.

Takteinteilung, ohne (G.) Without being divided into measures, without bar lines.

talon, au (F.) At the frog end of the bow.

talone, al (It.) Same as TALON, AU.

tambor con tirantes de cuerdas (Sp.) Snare drum.

tambour (F.) Drum.

tambour de Basque (F.) Tambourine.

tamburo (It.) Drum.

tan (Sp.) As much, e.g., *tan lento sea pueda,* as slowly as possible.

tändelnd (G.) Playful, flirting.

tanto (It.) Much, so much, as much, e.g., *allegro ma non tanto,* fast but not too much so.

tänzerisch (G.) Dancelike. Also, **tanzhaft.**

Tanzzeitmass (G.) Dance tempo.

tapado (Sp.) Muffled.

tardo (It.) (1) Slow, serious. (2) Late, delayed.

tasto (It.) (1) Fingerboard, e.g., *sul tasto,* over the fingerboard. Also, **sulla tastiera.** (2) Key. (3) Fret.

tautino (It.) Stubborn, bull-like.

tavola, sulla (It.) Over the belly (of violins, etc.).

t.c. (It.) Short for TRE CORDE.

Tem. I° (It.) Short for tempo primo (see PRIMA).

tema (It.) Theme, subject.

temperamentvoll (G.) Spirited, impulsive.

tempestoso (It.) Stormy, violent.

tempête, en (F.) Tempestuous, passionate.

tempo (It.) Time, rate of speed.

tempo, a (It.) Return to the original speed.

tempo di (It.) In the tempo of, e.g., *in tempo di menuetto,* in the tempo of a minuet.

Tempoveränderung (G.) Change of tempo.

temps (F.) Beat.

temps, en même (F.) At the same time.

ten. (It.) Short for TENUTO.

tenacemente (It.) Constantly, tenaciously.

Tendenz zur (G.) Tending toward, e.g., *Tendenz zur Ruhe,* tending to be soft.

tendrement (F.) Tenderly, lovingly. Also, **tendre.**

tenebroso (It.) Gloomy, somber.

teneramente (It.) Tenderly, gently. Also, **tenero, con tenerezza.**

tenido (Sp.) Held, sustained.

tenu (F.) Same as TENIDO.

tenuemente (Sp.) Slightly.

tenuto (It.) Held, sustained. Also, **tenuti, ten.**

teso (It.) Taut, tight, tense.

tetro (It.) Gloomy, dark, sad.

tibia (It., L.) In organs, an 8-foot open flute stop on the manuals.

tibia clausa (L.) In organs, an important stopped flute stop.

tibia plena (L.) In organs, a loud open 8-foot flute stop.

tibia profunda (It. + L.) In organs, a very low-pitched flute stop.

tibia sylvestris (L.) In organs, same as WALDFLÖTE.

tief (G.) (1) Deep, profound. (2) Low (in pitch).

tiefgesättigt (G.) Contented.

tiefschürfender Empfindung, mit (G.) With deep emotion.

tiempo (Sp.) Tempo, rate of speed.

tierce (F.) In organs, a rank of foundation pipes that sound two octaves and a third higher than the keys played. Also, **septadecima, seventeenth.**

timbales (F., Sp.) Timpani.

timbre (F.) Tone color.

timbro (It.) (1) Tone color. (2) The jingle of a tambourine.

timido (It.) Shy, bashful, hesitant. Also, **timidamente, con timidezza.**

timpani (It.) Kettledrums.

tirare in dietro (It.) To draw back.

tirasse (F.) Organ coupler, e.g., *sans tirasse,* pedal uncoupled.

tirata (It.) In vocal music, a slide or glide.

tirez (F.) Down-bow.

Todeslied (G.) A dirge, a lament. Also, **Todesgesang.**

todos (Sp.) All, everybody.

togliere la mano (It.) Remove the hand.

ton (F.) Tone, sound, pitch.

Ton (G.) Same as TON.

tonlos (G.) Toneless, monotonous.

tonvoll (G.) Tuneful, melodious.

torbido (It.) Gloomy, murky.

tornando (It.) Returning.

torrent, en (F.) Pouring out.

torturado (Sp.) Tortured, afflicted.

tosto, più (It.) See PIÙ TOSTO.

touche (F.) (1) Key (of a keyboard instrument), e.g., *touche noire,* black key, *touche blanche,* white key. (2) Fingerboard of a stringed instrument, e.g., *sur la touche,* (bow) over the fingerboard.

toujours (F.) Always, constantly.

tourbillonnant (F.) Whirling.

tous, tout, toute (F.) All, every, whole.

tr. (It.) Short for TRILLO.

träge (G.) Slow, lifeless.

tragico (It.) Tragic.

traîner (F.) To drag, to hold back, to slur. Also, **traîné.**

trait (F.) A rapid passage.

tranchant (F.) Sharp, cutting.

tranquille (F.) Quiet, peaceful, soft.

tranquillo (It.) Same as TRANQUILLE.

tranquilo (Sp.) Same as TRANQUILLE.

transfiguré (F.) Transfigured, changed.

trascinando (It.) Dragging, slowing down, drawing out the tone. Also, **trascinato, trascinare.**

trasfigurato (It.) Transformed, changed.

trasognato (It.) Daydreaming, half-asleep.

trasparente (It.) Clear, transparent.

trasporto (It.) (1) Joyful, rapturous. (2) Transposed.

trattenuto (It.) Held, sustained, slowed down.

Trauer, mit (G.) With sadness.

trauernd (G.) Mourning, grieving.

träumerisch (G.) Dreamy. Also, **traumhaft.**

traurig (G.) Sad, mournful.

Traversflöte (G.) Same as FLAUTO TRAVERSO.

tre (It.) Three, e.g., *a tre,* for three (parts).

tre corde (It.) Release the soft (una corda) pedal. Also, **tutte le corde, t.c.**

treibend (G.) Hurrying, pressing on. Also, **treiben.**

trem. (It.) Short for TREMOLO.

tremblant (F.) In organs, the tremulant.

tremblement (F.) (1) Trembling, quivering. (2) Trill.

tremolando (It.) Quivering, trembling, rippling.

tremolo (It.) A slight steady wavering of pitch. Also, **trem.**

trepidamente (It.) Anxious, fearful, trembling.

très (F.) Very, much.

trille (F.) Trill.

Triller (G.) Trill.

trillo (It.) Trill. Also, **tr.**

trinciante (It.) Cut up, separated, detached.

Triole (G.) Triplet.

triomphant (F.) Triumphant, exultant, rejoicing.

trionfale (It.) Exultant, victorious. Also, **trionfante.**

triple-croche (F.) Thirty-second note.

triste (F., It., Sp.) Sad, mournful, grieving. Also, (F.) **tristement,** (It.) **con tristezza,** (Sp.) **con tristeza.**

triumphierend (G.) Triumphant, exultant.

trocken (G.) Dry, precise, without feeling.

trois (F.) Three.

tromba (It.) (1) Trumpet, bugle. (2) In organs, a chorus reed stop.

trombón (Sp.) Trombone.

Trommel (G.) Drum.

trompa (Sp.) French horn.

trompeta (Sp.) Trumpet.

Trompete (G.) Trumpet.

trompette (F.) (1) Trumpet. (2) In organs, a loud chorus reed stop. Also, **French trumpet**.

trompette en chamade (F.) In organs, a chorus reed stop mounted in the front of the screen of the main organ or elsewhere, with the pipes in horizontal instead of vertical position. Also, **chamade, fan trumpet**.

trompette harmonique (F.) In organs, a very powerful 8-foot chorus reed stop.

tronco (It.) Cut short, abrupt.

trop (F.) Too, too much.

troppo (It.) Too, too much, e.g., *lento ma non troppo*, slow but not too slow.

trottinant, en (F.) At a regular rapid pace.

touche (F.) (1) Fingerboard (of violins, etc.). (2) Fret (of lutes, viols, etc.). (3) Key (of pianos, organs, etc.).

trüb (G.) Gloomy, sad.

tuba (1) (It., Sp.) Tuba, bass tuba. (2) (It.) Old name for trumpet. (3) (L.) Trumpet. (4) (It., L.) In organs, a name for various chorus reed stops with a firmer tone quality than the trompette or trumpet stops.

tuba magna (It., L.) In organs, a loud, brilliant chorus reed stop.

tuba mirabilis (It.) In organs, a very loud and intensely brass-like 8-foot tuba stop.

tumultueux, tumultueuse (F.) Stormy, noisy.

tumultuoso (It.) Noisy, riotous, in an uproar.

turbulent (F.) Wild, stormy.

tutta, tutte, tutti (I.) (1) All, total, e.g., *tutta forza*, with all (i.e., the most possible) force, *tutte unite*, all together. (2) Full orchestra or full chorus (as opposed to the soloist).

tutte le corde (It.) Same as TRE CORDE.

U

über (G.) Over, above, e.g., *R.H. über L.H.*, right hand (crossing) over left hand.

Übergang (G.) Modulation, bridge.

übergehend (G.) Moving to, shading into, modulating.

übergreifen (G.) In keyboard music, to cross the hands, e.g., *L.H. übergreifen*, cross left hand over right.

überlegen (G.) Lofty, superior.

überleiten (G.) Effect a transition, modulate.

übermässig (G.) Excessive, immoderate.

Übermut, mit (G.) With high spirits, merrily, playfully. Also, **übermütig**.

überschwänglich (G.) Exuberantly.

übersetzen (G.) Cross over, e.g., *L.H. übersetzen*, cross left hand over (the right).

überströmend (G.) Overflowing, gushing, exultant.

übertrieben (G.) Exaggerated.

Überzeugung, mit (G.) With conviction.

u.c. (It.) Short for UNA CORDA.

udibile (It.) Audible.

uguale (It.) Equal, uniform, regular.

uguaglianza, con perfetta (It.) Perfectly even, perfectly uniform.

ugualmente (It.) Equally, just the same as.

ultima, ultimo (It.) The last.

um (G.) About, around, for, because of, e.g., *um ein geringes langsamer*, a little slower.

umore, con (It.) With humor, with wit.

un, une (F.) A, one.

un, una, uno (It.) A, one.

una corda (It.) Soft pedal. Also, **u.c.**

unaufdringlich (G.) Undemonstrative, unemphasized, colorless.

unaussprechbarem Entzücken, mit (G.) With unspeakable delight.

und (G.) And.

unda maris (L.) In organs, an undulating 8-foot stop made up of one or two ranks of pipes tuned slightly sharp or flat (if two ranks, one normal and one flat, or one sharp and one flat).

ungebunden (G.) Unrestrained, free.

ungeduldig (G.) Impatient. Also, **mit Ungeduld.**

ungefähr (G.) Approximate, approximately.

ungehemmt (G.) Unbounded, e.g., *mit ungehemmtem Entzücken*, with unbounded delight.

ungemein (G.) Extraordinarily, deeply, very.

ungestüm (G.) Violent, raging.

unhörbar (G.) Inaudible.

uni, unis (F.) Together, in unison.

uniforme (F.) Even, steady, regular.

unisono (It.) In unison, usually following a DIVISI section. Also, **all' unisono, unis., uniti.**

unmerklich (G.) Imperceptible.

unmutig (G.) Ill-humored, petulant, annoyed.

unregelmässig (G.) Uneven, irregular.

unruhig (G.) Restless.

unschuldig (G.) Innocent.

unstät (G.) Unsteady, restless, aimless.

unten (G.) Below, under, underneath. Also, **unter.**

Untersatz (G.) In organs, same as SOUBASSE.

unterstützend (G.) Supporting.

üppig (G.) Rich, full, lush.

urlando (It.) Howling, shouting, shrieking.

ursprünglich (G.) Original, e.g., *ursprüngliches Tempo*, original tempo.

V

va (It.) Go, go on.

vagamente (It.) Wandering, straying, drifting.

vagaroso (Sp.) Wandering, flitting.

vaghezza, con (It.) (1) With charm, gracefully. (2) Obsolete name for ornament.

vaghissimo (It.) Very vague, very uncertain.

vago (It.) Vague, uncertain.

vague (F.) (1) Vague, indefinite. (2) A wave or billow, a surge.

valeur (F.) Time value.

valeurs irrationelles (F.) Unequal time values.

vals (Sp.) Waltz.

valse (F.) Waltz.

vaporeux (F.) Airy, vague.

vaporoso (It.) Very light, airy, transparent.

variante (F., It.) A different version.

variazione (It.) Variation. Also, **var.**

veemente (It.) Intense, passionate.

véhémente (F.) Ardent, impetuous, emphatic.

velato (It.) Veiled, subdued.

vellutato (It.) Velvety, very smooth.

veloce (It.) Quite fast. Also, **velocemente, con velocità,** (F.) **véloce.**

veloz (Sp.) Fast.

vent, comme le (F.) Like the wind, light, airy.

verachtungsvoll (G.) Contemptuous, scornful.

Verbeugung, mit einer (G.) With a bow or curtsey.

verbreitern (G.) Broaden, similar to LARGO or LARGANDO.

verdianamente (It.) In the style of Verdi. Also, **verdiano.**

verdichten (G.) To condense, to speed up.

verdriesslich (G.) Peevish, vexed, depressed.

verdrossen (G.) Peevish, fretful, listless.

vergnügt (G.) Cheerful, merry.

verhallend (G.) Fading away.

verhaltener Stimme, mit (G.) In a low voice, in an undertone.

verhauchen (G.) (1) Exhale. (2) Dying away, with one's last breath.

verhauchend, ganz (G.) Expiring, dying away.

verhetzt (G.) Incited, aroused.

verinnerlicht (G.) Deepened, more intense, introspective.

verklärt (G.) Bright, radiant, transfigured.

verklingen (G.) To fade away. Also, **verklingend.**

verlangsamen (G.) To slow down.

verlassen (G.) To leave, to abandon.

verlierend (G.) Fading away.

verloren (G.) Hopeless, forlorn.

verlöschen (G.) Fade away, extinguish.

Verschiebung (G.) Soft pedal.

verschleiert (G.) Veiled, muffled.

verschwindend (G.) Disappearing, fading away.

versetzen (G.) To transpose.

versonnen (G.) Deeply thoughtful.

Verständnis, mit (G.) With insight, perceptively.

verstärken (G.) To swell, to become louder.

versunken (G.) Absorbed, preoccupied.

vertige, en un (F.) Dizzy, giddy. Also, **vertigineux.**

vertiginoso (It.) Dizzily, very fast.

verträumt (G.) Dreamy.

Verwandlung (G.) (1) Change, transformation. (2) Change of scene.

verweilend (G.) Delaying, slowing down, becoming broader.

verzögernd (G.) Delaying, holding back, retarding.

verzückt (G.) Ecstatic, enraptured.

verzweifelt (G.) Despairing. Also, **verzweiflungsvoll.**

vez, à la (Sp.) At the same time.

vezzoso (It.) Graceful, charming.

via (It.) Away, remove, e.g., *via le sordini,* remove the mutes.

vibrador (Sp.) Same as VIBRATO (1).

vibrant (F.) (1) Vibrating, sounding. (2) A vibrato.

vibrante (1) (It.) Forceful, vigorous. (2) (Sp.) Vibrating, trembling. Also, **vibrando.**

vibrar (Port.) To sound.

vibratissimo (It.) (1) Trembling, very agitated. (2) With a great deal of VIBRATO (1).

vibrato (It.) (1) Pulsation of musical sound. (2) Reverberating, resounding, ringing.

vibrieren lassen (G.) Continue to sound (i.e., do not mute or damp).

vicino (It.) Nearby, close.

vidalita (Sp.) A mournful love song.

vide (L.) See, indicating that the performer omit the notes between *vi-* and *-de.*

viel (G.) Much, a lot of, e.g., *mit viel Schwung,* with a lot of verve.

vieppiù (It.) Much more. Also, **viepiù.**

vier (G.) Four.

vierteilig (G.) Four-part.

Viertel (G.) Quarter note.

Viertelbewegung (G.) Literally, quarter-note rhythm, 4/4 time.

Vierundsechzigstel (G.) Sixty-fourth note.

vif (F.) Lively, animated. Also, **vivement.**

vigoroso (It.) Vigorously, boldly, energetically. Also, **con vigore.**

vigoureusement (F.) Energetic, forceful.

viol, viola (Sp.) Viola.

viola d'amore (It.) (1) An older instrument of the violin group. (2) In organs, a soft string stop.

viole à pavillon (F.) In organs, a string stop of unusually bright but delicate tone.

viole conique (F.) In organs, an 8-foot string stop resembling the tone of a soft violin. Also, **viole sordine,** (It.) **violino sordo.**

viole d'orchestre (F.) In organs, an important string stop. Also, **orchestral violin, violin.**

violento (Sp.) Impulsive, furious.

violenza, colla (It.) Vehemently, with force.

violetta (It.) In organs, a loud brilliant string stop.

violín (Sp.) Violin.

violino (It.) Violin.

violino da spalla (It.) Concertmaster.

violon (F.) Violin.

violón (Sp.) Double bass.

violoncelle (F.) Cello.

violoncello (It.) (1) Cello. (2) In organs, an important string stop with the tone of the orchestral cello. Also, **cello.**

violoncelo (Sp.) Cello.

violone (It.) (1) Contrabass viol. (2) In organs, same as CONTRA VIOLONE.

virtuoso (It.) Brilliant, technically very difficult.

visionär (G.) Visionary.

visionario (It.) Visionary.

vista, a (It.) At sight, sightreading. Also, **a prima vista.**

vita, più (It.) Livelier, more animated.

vite (F.) Fast, rapid. Also, **vitement, vitesse.**

viv. (It.) Short for VIVACE.

vivace (It.) A lively tempo, somewhat faster than ALLEGRO.

vivement (F.) Same as VIF.

vivezza, con (It.) Lively, brisk, animated.

vivido (It.) Lively, vigorous.

vivo (Sp.) Lively, intense.

vni. (It.) Short for violins.

voglia, con (It.) Longingly, eagerly.

voilé (F.) Also, **voilée.** (1) Veiled, subdued. (2) In singing, a husky tone.

voix (F.) Voice or voice-part.

voix blanche (F.) A light pure tone, with relatively few overtones.

voix céleste (F.) In organs, an 8-foot string stop of undulating tone, usually made up of two ranks of salicional pipes, one tuned normal and the other slightly sharp or slightly flat. Also, **céleste, vox céleste.**

voix humaine (F.) In organs, same as VOX HUMANA.

voix intérieure (F.) Inner voice-part.

volando (It.) Flying, skimming rapidly.

volante (It.) Rushing, rapid.

volée, à toute (F.) Vibrating fully.

volgare (It.) Coarse, unrefined, common, popular.

volgare, con (It.) In the vernacular.

Volkston, im (G.) Colloquially, popular, folklike.

volkstümlich (G.) Also, **volksthümlich.** (1) National, ethnic. (2) Popular.

voll (G.) Full, fully, completely.

vollem Ton, mit (G.) With a full tone.

vollständig (G.) Completely, wholly. Also, **vollkommen.**

volonté, à (F.) Freely, at the performer's discretion.

volta (It.) Time, e.g., *prima volta*, first time.

volteggiando (It.) Crossing (hands).

volti subito (It.) Turn the page quickly. Also, **v.s.**

volubile (F.) Fluent, flowing.

volubilità, con (It.) Fickle, highly changeable, inconstant.

volubilmente (It.) Fluent, flowing, rapid.

volupté, avec (F.) Full, rich, luxurious.

voluttuoso (It.) Luxuriously, sensuously.

vom (G.) From the, e.g., *vom Anfang*, from the beginning.

von (G.) From, e.g., *von fern*, from a distance.

vontade, a (Port.) At the performer's discretion.

vor (G.) Before, in front of, previous to.

voran (G.) (1) Before, ahead, in front. (2) Go on, continue.

vorangehen (G.) Preceding, leading, continuing.

vorbereiten (G.) To prepare in advance (with regard to organ stops, etc.).

Vorhang (G.) Curtain (of stage), e.g., *Vorhang auf*, raise the curtain.

vorher (G.) Before, previously.

vorig, vorige, voriger (G.) Former, previous, foregoing, e.g., *voriger Satz*, previous movement.

vor sich hin (G.) In front of one, forward.

Vortrag (G.) Style of delivery, execution, e.g., *frei im Vortrag*, in a free style.

vorwärts (G.) Go on, continue without pause. Also, **vorwärtsgehen**.

vorwurfsvoll (G.) Reproachful.

vorzutragen (G.) To perform, to present.

vox (L.) Voice or voice-part.

vox acuta (L.) In organs, same as ACUTA.

vox angelica (L.) In organs, an 8-foot stop that represents the softest single rank of pipes.

vox céleste (L. + F.) Same as VOIX CÉLESTE.

vox gravissima (L. + It.) In organs, same as GRAVISSIMA.

vox humana (L. + It.) In organs, an important reed stop. Also, **Menschenstimme, voix humaine**.

vox mystica (L.) In organs, the softest reed stop.

voz (Sp.) Voice or voice-part.

v.s. (It.) Short for VOLTI SUBITO.

vuota (It.) Open, e.g., *corda vuota*, open string.

W

wachsend (G.) Growing louder.

wählerisch (G.) Fastidious, dainty, choosy.

Waldflöte (G.) In organs, an open, moderately loud flute stop. Also, **Feldflöte**, (L.) **tibia sylvestris**.

Waldhorn (G.) In organs, a reed stop designed to sound like a hunting horn. Also, (F.) **cor de chasse**, (It.) **corno di caccia, hunting horn**.

wallend (G.) Boiling, simmering.

Walzer (G.) Waltz.

Walzerzeitmass (G.) Waltz time.

Wärme, mit (G.) With warmth, with feeling.

wechselnd (G.) Changing, e.g., *in wechselndem Tempo*, in changing tempo.

weg (G.) Away, off, e.g., *Dämpfer weg*, without mute.

Weh, mit (G.) With pain, lamenting.

wehmütig (G.) Sad, melancholy.

weich (G.) Soft, gentle.

weichflüssig (G.) Sweetly flowing.

weihevoll (G.) Worshipful, solemn. Also, **mit Weihe.**

weinerlich (G.) Weepy, tearful. Also, **weinend.**

weiterklingen (G.) Continuing to sound.

weltentrückt (G.) Solitary, withdrawn.

wenig (G.) Little.

weniger (G.) Less.

werden (G.) To become, e.g., *leise werden,* become soft.

wesentlich (G.) (1) Fundamental, basic. (2) Chiefly, essentially.

wie (G.) As, e.g., *wie vorher,* as before, *wie zu Beginn,* as in the beginning.

wieder (G.) Again.

Wiederholung (G.) Repeat.

wiegend (G.) Rocking, swaying rhythmically.

wild (G.) Tumultuous, passionate.

wirbelnd (G.) (1) Warbling. (2) Sounding a drumroll.

wuchtig (G.) Ponderous, slow.

wühlend (G.) Violent.

würdig (G.) Stately, dignified. Also, **mit Würde.**

wütend (G.) Furious, enraged.

X

xilófono (Sp.) Xylophone.

Y

y (Sp.) And.

Z

zaghaft (G.) Shy, timid, wavering.

zänkisch (G.) Quarrelsome, scolding.

zart (G.) Tender, delicate, soft. Also, **mit Zartheit, zärtlich.**

Zartflöte (G.) In organs, an open flute stop of subdued tone.

Zauberflöte (G.) In organs, a stopped flute stop, moderately soft and of very clear tone.

zeffiroso (It.) Very light and airy.

Zeit (G.) (1) Time, a pause. (2) Tempo.

Zeit lassen (G.) (1) Perform freely (with regard to tempo). (2) Allow for a pause.

Zeitmass (G.) Tempo.

ziemlich (G.) Rather, quite, e.g., *ziemlich schnell,* quite fast.

zierlich (G.) Dainty, graceful, elegant.

Zimbel (G.) (1) Cymbal. (2) In organs, a brilliant mixture stop made up of open metal foundation pipes. Also, **cymbal.**

Zimbelflöte (G.) In organs, same as CAMPANA (3).

Zink (G.) (1) The obsolete cornett (wind instrument). (2) In organs, a pedal reed stop.

zitternd (G.) Trembling.

zögernd (G.) Hesitating, holding back.

zornig (G.) Angry.

zu (G.) (1) To. (2) Too, e.g., *nicht zu langsam*, not too slow.

zufrieden (G.) Satisfied, contented, peaceful.

zügig (G.) Spirited, fiery.

zum (G.) To the, e.g., *bis zum Schluss*, to the end.

zunehmend (G.) (1) Increasing, e.g., *mit zunehmender Leidenschaft*, with increasing passion. (2) Growing louder.

Zungenschlag (G.) Tonguing.

zurückhalten (G.) To hold back, to slow down.

zurückkehrend (G.) Returning.

zurücknehmen (G.) To withdraw.

zurücksinkend (G.) Falling back, relapsing.

zurücktreten (G.) To retreat, to become softer.

zuversichtlich (G.) Confident, hopeful.

zuvor, als (G.) As before.

zwanglos (G.) Unconstrained, free.

zwei (G.) Two.

zweiteilig (G.) Two-part.

Zweiunddreissigstel (G.) Thirty-second note.

zwischen (G.) Between.

Zwischenspiel (G.) Interlude, intermezzo.

Zwischenvorhang (G.) Drop curtain.

Christine Ammer, born in Austria, was editor of the *Harvard Dictionary of Music* (1969) and is the author of *Harper's Dictionary of Music* (1972) and *Unsung: A History of Women in American Music* (1980).